Praise for The *P*

"When the passion dies, the marriage often follows. So many will never divorce and remain miserably married. *The Passion Principles* is a great guide to restore the passion or to build on whatever is there. The end result for those who follow the passion principles is a full and rich marriage that starts in that sacred place known as the bedroom."

—STEPHEN ARTERBURN
TALK-RADIO HOST; SPEAKER; AND AUTHOR, *THE EXCEPTIONAL LIFE*

"This is a book I will recommend to every newlywed couple with whom I work. Shannon beautifully addresses the most difficult questions about sex in a very practical and easy-to-read way. But she goes further, by continuously pointing back to its very design. This book will free you to realize how honoring God and having great sex go hand-in-hand."

—JOSHUA STRAUB, PhD
COAUTHOR, *GOD ATTACHMENT*

"Shannon has provided powerful, practical tools for couples to experience a healthy sexual balance, to feel safe and sexy in the privacy of their own bedrooms. What a great gift to couples for creating many moments of passion and pleasure as God intended."

—DR. CATHERINE HART WEBER
COAUTHOR, *SECRETS OF EVE*

"Wow! From the very *basic* basics to the cherry-on-top extras, Shannon Ethridge talks *sex*. This bold, honest, and frank book will empower many, who take the time to read and apply, to discover the sacred fun and freedom God has created for marriages."

—ELISA MORGAN
PUBLISHER, FULLFILL; SPEAKER; AUTHOR, *THE BEAUTY OF BROKEN*;
AND MOPS INTERNATIONAL PRESIDENT EMERITA

"What I love about Shannon Ethridge is that she gives you the truth, based on knowledge, full of wisdom, and spoken in love. She says what everyone else is hesitant to say but needs to hear. Her passion for her topic can fire up your passion for your spouse and for Christ!"

—Kathy Floyd, M. A., LPC
Speaker and women's ministry leader

"Finally! It was like a breath of fresh air reading Shannon's latest book, *The Passion Principles: Celebrating Sexual Freedom in Marriage*. Not only did she hit all of the hot and vital topics, but she also dove deep into Scripture and God's amazing plan for healthy sexuality. There is great freedom as well as blessings for sex in marriage, and sadly many of us have a skewed view. Thank you, Shannon, for writing a book that is full of grace, freedom, and encouragement that lines up perfectly with God's plan!"

—Brad & Kate Aldrich
Cofounders, OneFleshMarriage.com

"As I paid for my movie ticket, I was given a pair of glasses guaranteed to transform the animated feature from 2-D to 3-D. Shannon Ethridge has given us more. She has provided us with information capable of transforming the knowledge of human sexuality into 4-dimensions . . . the spiritual, mental, emotional, and physical. *The Passion Principles* is capable of increasing not only your knowledge but also the joy and pleasure you experience in your marriage."

—Kendra Smiley
Speaker and author, *Live Free* and
Journey of a Strong-Willed Child

"While the church remains mostly silent about healthy sexuality, *The Passion Principles* is a burst of oxygen for those suffocating in the void of information. It is a treasure chest of truth awaiting those who long for intimate connection and sexual fulfillment. Compassionate, open, practical, and brilliantly insightful—thank you Shannon!"

—Steve and Holly Holladay
Founders, Ultimate Escape

THE
PASSION
PRINCIPLES

Celebrating Sexual Freedom in Marriage

Shannon Ethridge

W Publishing Group

AN IMPRINT OF THOMAS NELSON

Published in Nashville, Tennessee, by W Publishing Group, an imprint of Thomas Nelson.

Thomas Nelson titles may be purchased in bulk for educational, business, fund-raising, or sales promotional use. For information, please e-mail SpecialMarkets @ThomasNelson.com.

Names and facts from stories contained in this book have been changed, but the emotional and sexual struggles portrayed are true stories as related to the author through personal interviews, letters, or e-mails. Permission has been granted for use of real names, stories, and correspondence with some individuals.

Any Internet address, phone number, or company or product information printed in this book is offered as a resource and is not intended in any way to be or to imply an endorsement by Thomas Nelson, nor does Thomas Nelson vouch for the existence, content, or services of these sites, phone numbers, companies, or products beyond the life of this book.

Unless otherwise noted, Scripture quotations are taken from the *Holy Bible*, New Living Translation. © 1996, 2004, 2007. Used by permission of Tyndale House Publishers, Inc., Wheaton, Illinois 60189. All rights reserved.

Other Scripture quotations are from the Good News Translation (GNT). ©1976, 1992 by the American Bible Society. Used by permission. All rights reserved. New Century Version® (NCV). © 2005 by Thomas Nelson, Inc. Used by permission. All rights reserved; Holy Bible, New International Version®, NIV® (NIV). © 1973, 1978, 1984, 2011 by Biblica, Inc.™ Used by permission of Zondervan. All rights reserved worldwide; New King James Version® (NKJV). © 1982 by Thomas Nelson, Inc. Used by permission. All rights reserved; and *The Message* by Eugene H. Peterson. © 1993, 1994, 1995, 1996, 2000, 2001, 2002. Used by permission of NavPress Publishing Group.

Library of Congress Cataloging-in-Publication Data

Ethridge, Shannon.
   The passion principles : celebrating sexual freedom in marriage / Shannon Ethridge.
      pages cm
Includes bibliographical references.
   ISBN 978-0-8499-6447-3 (trade paper)
1. Sex—Religious aspects—Christianity. 2. Marriage—Religious aspects—
Christianity. I. Title.
BT708.E846 2013
241'.664—dc23

                                                                         2013025862

Printed in the United States of America
14 15 16 17 18 RRD 6 5 4 3 2 1

To Greg

*Thank you for teaching me how to make love
with so much more than just my body.*

Contents

PASSION PRINCIPLE #1:
CELEBRATE THE SPIRITUAL SIDE OF SEX

PLAYING BY THE RULE BOOK

PASSION PRINCIPLE #2:
CELEBRATE THE MENTAL SIDE OF SEX

SEX ON THE BRAIN

GETTING ON THE SAME PAGE

RULES OF (MENTAL) ENGAGEMENT

MOVING FORWARD MENTALLY

Passion Principle #3:
Celebrate the Emotional Side of Sex

MOVING BEYOND ABUSE

MOVING BEYOND BETRAYAL

EVOLUTION OF A RELATIONSHIP

Passion Principle #4:
Celebrate the Physical Side of Sex

HYGIENE 101

EUREKA!

LET FREEDOM RING!

SHANNON'S QUESTION TO *YOU*

Acknowledgments

IT IS AN AWESOME AND HUMBLING EXPERIENCE TO WATCH A BOOK evolve from start to finish. So many people invest their time, energies, and talents, and the finished product bears many fingerprints. Those that touched this project and touched my heart in the process are numerous.

First, thanks to Debbie Wickwire and the entire W Publishing Group for sharing my vision for this book. Not only are you amazing professionals, you are simply wonderful people who represent God well.

So many of my B.L.A.S.T. mentorship program graduates rolled up their sleeves and tirelessly combed through multitudes of pages, wielding red pens with great courage and skill. Maureen Brown, Andrew Clark, Kathy Floyd, Suze Hamel, Will Health, Carol Henders, Christy Kennard, Jodi Kozan, Rebecca Larson, Cindy Palin, Megan Reuwer, Charissa Steyn, and Rich Wildman—thank you for eagerly polishing these pages with me. It was a delightful collaborative effort!

Two very special men in my life made sure I was writing to *both* genders, not just women, at every turn. Greg and Jim, thank you for your uniquely male perspectives and the multitude of ways you contributed, edited, and encouraged me throughout the process.

Much of the fodder contained in this book came directly from readers and coaching clients who have shared their stories with me over the past decade. What a privilege to be invited to share in your journeys as you have sought to fully blossom sexually, emotionally, and spiritually. May your honest questions, comments, and testimonies be an inspiration to many other couples.

Foreword

Eat, lovers, and drink
until you are drunk with love!
—Song of Songs 5:1 GNT

THERE IS A REASON GOD HIMSELF URGES US TO FEAST ON SEXUAL intimacy, to allow ourselves to become intoxicated with the pleasure of marital passion. In the language of football, the best defense is often a good offense.

In my book *Pure Pleasure* I tell the story of one of my first runs in Houston, Texas, where I now live. I landed in America's fourth-largest city in the middle of August, flying in from Seattle, where a heat wave is defined as five hours with temperatures eighty degrees and above. You would be hard-pressed to find five hours in Houston's summertime when the temperature ever drops *below* eighty degrees.

In my naive foolishness I set off for a six-mile run in the thick of the afternoon, when the sun was at its highest. Even more foolish, I neglected to bring water—I would *never* carry water for a six-mile run in Seattle.

Within fifteen minutes I realized my mistake. It was as if someone had blown a hair dryer straight down my throat. After about thirty minutes I passed a half-empty bottle of Coke lying in a ditch, practically boiling in the sun.

I actually paused.

It was gross beyond description, but at least it was wet, and I needed something wet.

Gary, I said to myself, *you can't fall that far.* Leaving the Coke where it was, I traveled another stretch until I realized my situation was nearly life-threatening. I saw a woman playing with her children in their front yard, a garden hose rolled up in front of the house.

With great embarrassment I asked the woman if I could take a drink. She could not have been more pleasant. Feeling ashamed that I was interrupting this family's afternoon, I wanted to get out of there as soon as possible, so I quickly turned on the faucet and immediately lifted the hose to my lips.

As that toxic, bacteria encrusted hot stream poured down my throat, a little voice in the back of my head warned me, *Gary, you are so going to regret this. This water will make you so sick that in three hours, you'll likely wish you were dead.*

But here's the thing: I didn't care. I was so thirsty that I was more than willing to face terrible consequences three hours later. I just needed a drink *now*.

You could fault my lack of self-control, but wouldn't it be wiser to ask why had I let myself get so thirsty that something that should have been repugnant to me—a half-empty bottle of Coke lying in a ditch, water that had been boiling in a rubber hose for days—had actually become a temptation?

Shannon Ethridge gets it. She realizes that it is far more

beneficial to address the state of thirst than to try to exist on iron-willed self-control, which is why she has written a book that pours pure, nourishing, and unpolluted water straight into our souls.

In a world where so much teaching on sex is convoluted and cowardly, Shannon Ethridge is refreshingly bold and clear. Her expressive language may stretch some of us to the point of discomfort, but I believe Shannon is a spiritual poet, reaching to find new and effective ways to challenge us. She insists that we look with a holy but honest eye at the raw reality yet resplendent glory of human sexuality. She is an enthusiastic writer and an equally enthusiastic and bold thinker. Such writers usually start conversations, and such conversations usually start controversies. But it is out of this process we can emerge wiser, more intimate, and more like Christ.

Applying Shannon's book will do far more than merely improve our sex lives. It will help our marriages on all levels. You see, I believe it is in God's kindness that it is so difficult to maintain long-term sexual intimacy in marriage after the initial sexual chemistry has faded. This difficulty, quite frankly, is why so many couples all but give up and allow their sexual relationships to resemble a distant relative who visits only on major holidays. It takes commitment, effort, and intention to keep this blessing of God flowing freely. If we are going to continue to enjoy and serve each other sexually in our second and third decades of marriage as much as, or even more than, we did in the first decade, we will be forced to talk, to grow in humility, to learn how to listen and understand and have sometimes embarrassing and painful conversations.

Now, consider this: *these are the very skills needed for a marriage to succeed on all levels.* If you grow in humility, if you learn how to listen, if you develop courage to bring something up instead of cowardly keeping silent, and if you create a marital climate where even the potentially embarrassing facets of life can be looked at under a microscope, there isn't an element of your marriage that won't benefit from these newly enhanced relational skills.

That is why this book, seemingly focused on sex, has the potential to improve your marriage in all aspects. It will launch new conversations. It will spur you to new levels of self-disclosure. You will be inspired to forgive and to ask for forgiveness. Shannon urges you to have empathy for your spouse instead of pity for yourself. As a crowning achievement *The Passion Principles* invites you to understand God more fully, worship Him more enthusiastically, and become a little more like Christ.

What more could you ask of a book than that?

You may not accept every one of Shannon's points. You may well challenge some of her poetic descriptions, but you will be transformed in the way one is always inspired by spending time in the presence of an extraordinarily energetic artist.

Allow Shannon to teach you how to drink deeply of the pure water of holy marital passion, and neither you nor your spouse will have to live in this pornographic world with a dangerous thirst.

Eat your fill, O lovers; be drunk with love.

—Gary Thomas
Author of *Sacred Marriage* and *The Sacred Search*

Introduction

OVER THE PAST TWENTY-FOUR YEARS OF MARRIAGE AND MINIS-
try, I have often wondered if I have a neon sign on my forehead
that reads: "Tell me about your sex life!"

Everywhere I go, every country I visit, it is usually what
people eventually wind up talking to me about. It is weird, or so
I have been told. But I have grown used to it. And I have even
become very grateful for it. I feel as if I am being invited into the
inner sanctum of people's deepest struggles, darkest secrets, and
most embarrassing questions. To be such a trusted confidant is an
overwhelming privilege—one I do not take lightly.

One of the key things I have come to realize is that marital
tension is most often created when one partner's views on sexuality swing a little too far to the left (too liberal) or a little too
far to the right (too conservative) to suit his or her spouse. Either
extreme is unhealthy at best, downright destructive at worst.
Given that sexual incompatibility is one of the most common
sources of marital tension and the driving factor behind many
divorces, we cannot deny the power our sexual viewpoints hold.
That is why it is so vital that couples get on the same page sexually—and stay there.

My desire is to help all married couples—both wives and husbands, newlyweds and not-so-newlyweds—experience a healthy sexual balance so they can feel safe and sexy in the privacy of their own bedrooms. Because . . .

> when you have two sexually healthy spouses, you have a
> strong marriage.
> when you have a strong marriage, you have a strong family.
> when you have a strong family, you have a strong
> community.
> when you have a strong community, you have a strong
> society.

So I guess you could say that this book is my contribution to society . . . in my own weird sort of way.

This book is divided into four sections—four passion principles—and contains forty bite-sized, easy-to-digest (even-right-before-bedtime) readings. At the end of some of these readings, you will find a few "Ponder the Principle" questions to contemplate alone or to use as conversation starters if you are reading this together as a couple. At other times I offer a prayer at the end of the reading that you can meditate on, either alone or together. And some readings I simply wrap up as a gift that will hopefully keep giving and giving as you grow closer and closer in the days ahead.

I pray these passion principles rock your marriage (and your marriage bed) for many years to come.

SHANNON

PASSION PRINCIPLE #1:

Celebrate the Spiritual Side of Sex

One + One = One

1. ■ WHAT WAS GOD THINKING WHEN HE CREATED SEX?

SEX IS THE MOST SCANDALOUS, SINFUL, SHAMEFUL THING IN THE world . . . so be sure to save it for someone you love.

If we are honest, this is the mind-set of far too many Christians, whether we recognize it or not. Most of us were raised by well-intentioned parents and church leaders who wanted the best for us, so they attempted to "sanitize" our thinking about all things sexual.

For example, growing up I heard more than a few sermons or youth group lessons about how destructive sex can be . . . how sex should be avoided at all costs . . . how sex is Satan's favorite tool to use to bring Christians to their knees (and not in a good way). But I never heard a sermon about how beautiful, powerful, and pleasurable sex within marriage is . . . how a husband and wife should freely indulge in sex as often as possible . . . about how God can reveal Himself through healthy sexual intimacy in ways that absolutely blow our minds (to an even greater degree than the proverbial mind-blowing orgasm).

Another common scenario is that we were raised in families and churches that said nothing at all about sex, leaving us to draw our conclusions mainly from peers, music, magazines, romance novels, TV, and the Internet. With such teachers, we learned that the human sex drive is about as controllable as a raging waterfall or stoppable as a freight train . . . that if we want to have good, hot sex, we had better do it while we are single because once we are married we won't be getting any . . . that the forbidden fruit of an extramarital affair tastes far sweeter than simply savoring the spouse to whom you have committed your life.

So many sex-negative messages, so few sex-positive messages. How in the world are we to see sexuality through a crystal-clear lens? How can we recognize the goodness and perfection of what God had in mind when He created sex in the first place?

That is the challenge of this book—and one that I am grateful to have the opportunity to tackle—because, quite frankly, if Christian couples cannot have phenomenal sex lives given the personal spiritual connection we have with the Author and Originator of sex, then who in the world can? But because sex is such a touchy subject with many Christians, I most likely will offend you at some point in this book although that is certainly not my intention. I only ask that you *not* throw out the baby with the bathwater. (Feel free to get a Sharpie marker and black out any sentences that ruffle too many of your feathers, but keep reading anyway.)

It is easy to tell when a man or a woman has been indoctrinated into a sex-negative way of thinking simply by the words that come out of his or her mouth:

- Tina, age 23, who just six weeks before her wedding day posed the question, "Does a marriage really have to involve sex? I mean, I know I'll need to have sex to conceive children, but other than that, I'm really hoping my husband will be satisfied with just living happily together because the idea of him putting 'that thing' inside of me makes me nauseous." (Obviously no one has told Tina that intercourse is the most natural and pleasurable thing known to man— and woman.)

- Carla, 54, who declared after almost thirty years of marriage, "Every time my husband touches me, I feel used and abused. I've told him many times that if he can't leave me alone, I can't stay married to him." (And the shocking thing about this situation is that Carla is married to an ordained minister. Not even an experienced spiritual leader with a PhD in theology has found the words to help her embrace God's gift of sexual intimacy in marriage.)

- Pamela, 36, who insists, "My husband wants to look at me naked with the lights on, but I can't stand the thought." (Do women really think they can starve their husbands' appetites for visual stimulation by hiding behind frumpy clothes and fuzzy pajamas? Why can't we just get comfortable baring all in the bedroom?)

- Brenda, 27, who says, "I always thought men wanted sex all the time, and that women typically rejected such advances. It's the other way around at my house, and I'm wondering how I *cannot* take his lack of sexual interest personally." (I know from dozens of e-mails I receive each week that Brenda is not alone with her sexual frustration and feelings of rejection.)

You may think it is only women who are sexually confused and frustrated. Think again. Here are a few snippets from men:

- Brandon, age 29, who complains, "I keep asking my wife what she wants in bed to become a more interested sex partner, but she has offered little in the way of guidance. I want to be her 'dream lover,' but I can't read her mind." (Why does sexual communication have to be so awkward? Why don't we have the vocabulary skills to discuss our most common denominator—that we all are sexual beings?)
- Craig, 37, who admitted, "I simply don't desire sex nearly as often as my wife, and I suspect that makes me a freak of nature, especially when compared to the stereotypical horny guy. If men are the ones who supposedly want sex all the time and women are the disinterested ones, then what does that make me?" (How sad that Craig compares himself to stereotypes, and that such comparisons lead to feelings of emasculation.)
- Kirk, 45, who says, "My wife has no idea that I go to bed absolutely burning with passion for her practically every night. If I admitted that, she'd surely feel 'put upon' or that I am some sort of animal. I settle for once a week out of fear that she might cut me off completely." (How horrifying to imagine that some men feel as if they are broken or dysfunctional for simply wanting what God wired them to desire.)

Is *this* what God intended when He created sex? That wives would feel fearful, abused, put upon, objectified, rejected?

That husbands would feel inadequate, frustrated, emasculated, animalistic?

No, it is not. It is absolutely, positively *not* what He had in mind.

How do I know?

I know God. Granted, He did not appear to me in the flesh and sit down over a cup of tea as I was crafting this book. But because He has given us His Word, we can certainly know His character and nature—which is to bless, not to burden . . . to protect, not to punish . . . to delight, not to discourage. And I believe His gift of sexuality is intended to bring us overwhelming pleasure, not intense pain . . . to fascinate, not to frustrate . . . to add and multiply good things into our lives and relationships, not subtract and divide.

But how do we make that transition from sex-negative thinking to sex-positive thinking so we can enjoy such a grand and glorious gift? How do we go from hypervigilant self-protection to freely sharing our minds, bodies, hearts, and souls with one another as God intended? How do we enjoy our one-flesh union so that we are captivated, mesmerized, and blissful, as if we are one step away from heaven's door? While there is no established formula for accomplishing such a paradigm shift, I would like to tell you about a pivotal experience in my life that opened up all kinds of mental, emotional, and spiritual pathways through which I could more fully embrace the physical side of my sexuality without feeling like a "bad girl."

I was working toward my master's degree in counseling/human relationships at Liberty University when my human sexuality professor, Dr. David Lawson, posed this shocking question to the class:

"How is your relationship with God *sexual* in nature?"

Silence. All of us students sat there at our desks wondering, *Is this a joke?*

It was no joke. It was our honest-to-goodness, serious-as-a-heart-attack assignment to discuss this deep theological question in a small-group setting for the following two hours.

Two hours? *Wouldn't two* minutes *be enough?* I thought.

Little did I realize that we could have chewed on this topic for two full days and still not have exhausted all the possibilities. Our small group tossed around all kinds of insightful responses, such as the fact that in both our sexual relationships with our spouses and spiritual relationships with God there is:

· trust	· vulnerability	· genuine interest
· full acceptance	· deep desire	· true communion
· closeness	· connection	· life-giving transference
· openness	· honesty	· humility
· risk	· intimacy	· passion
· purpose	· pleasure	· transcendence
· euphoria	· completion	· synergy

As I have continued to contemplate this question and even discuss it with audience members at some of my speaking events, I have realized that our sexuality serves all kinds of amazing purposes. Before we even look at Scripture (which we will dive into in the next few questions), just consider: what else in all of creation can so effectively . . .

- comfort you when you are sad?
- calm you when you are anxious?
- provide an outlet for expression when you are excited?
- relieve boredom?
- help you forget your current trials and tribulations?

- make you sleep better?
- provide intense, guilt-free pleasure?
- help you feel deeply connected to another human being *and* to God?
- erase feelings of loneliness and isolation?
- give you an interesting break from your daily routine?
- relieve stress and even certain aches and pains?
- enhance your overall health and vitality?
- fulfill your hopes and dreams of parenthood?
- rev your engine, float your boat, light your fire?
- send sparks through your brain and shivers down your spine?
- make you feel so giddy, so special, so cherished and celebrated?

Yeah, only sex can do all that. And it does all that quite well!

So what was God thinking when He created sex? I believe He was thinking, *I am going to make their day . . . and their nights too!*

If we grasped these concepts fully, how would it change our sex lives? Our spiritual lives? Our marriages? Our family dynamics? Could we learn to see sexuality as the tremendous gift that God surely intended? Would we be inspired to give God all the more thanks and praise in our daily lives? Would we experience even more passion and pleasure as we fully allow ourselves to get caught up in the rapturous experience of fully loving and affirming one another?

All of that and more is possible. And instead of sounding like any of the individuals previously mentioned in this chapter, perhaps you will begin to sound a lot more like:

- Cindi, who declared publicly in her Sunday school class, "I love the fact that my husband is a wonderful spiritual leader, provider, and father, but what I really love most about Jeff is that he is a *great lover.*"
- Nick, who stated with tears in his eyes in a recent coaching session, "The highlight of my day is coming home to my wife. To me, she just oozes sex appeal, and it's so easy to forget all of my problems from work and get lost in her love for me."
- Ruth, who was asked by a nurse if she would like a one year's supply of free condoms. When she responded positively, the nurse asked how many exactly would she need. Ruth stated matter-of-factly, "Three hundred and sixty-five." (I'm guessing it wasn't a leap year.)

To be held in high regard as a "great lover," to feel "lost" in one another, to assume that you can be sexually intimate with your spouse on any given day that you desire without fear of rejection . . . *Wow!* Who *doesn't* want that?

So enjoy this journey of exploring the spiritual, mental, emotional, and physical dimensions of our sexuality, celebrating the many freedoms that Christians have in the marriage bed, and learn to incorporate these passion principles into our relationships so that we can enjoy this gift to the fullest.

PONDER THE PRINCIPLE

What kind of sex-negative messages have you received in life? What were the sources of such messages, and in hindsight, how reliable were those sources or the information they provided?

🔥 Are you ready to reject any view of sexuality that doesn't measure up to the passionate, pleasurable acts of intimacy that God intended for married couples to enjoy? Why or why not?

🔥 If you are reading this along with your spouse, will you commit to one another to keep reading this book all the way through to the end so you can both develop the healthiest sexual mind-set possible?

2. WHY DOES GOD SAY WE HAVE TO BE MARRIED TO HAVE SEX?

I have received a few e-mails over the past two decades from people insisting that the Bible doesn't expressly forbid sex between two consenting adults. Funny how this question is always posed by single people—most likely sexually active single people is my best guess—but never by married people, and certainly never by married people who have really great, God-fearing, earth-shaking, soul-stirring sex lives. I think those couples totally get it. But since this is such a common question, let's go there for a moment.

While you won't find a passage that says, "Thou shalt not have sex prior to marriage," you will find scriptures that address the seriousness of "fornication" (sex between two people who aren't married to each other) as well as a commandment against "adultery" (sex between a married person and someone who is not his or her spouse). We will discuss some of those scriptures later in this section, but for now let's just take a look at Genesis 2:24, which I think explains what God envisioned when He created both marriage and sex (in that order): "This explains why a man leaves his father and mother and is joined to his wife, and the two are united into one."

Notice that there is a distinct sequence to this passage:

- First, a man will leave his father and mother *completely*—no boomeranging back. He will prepare to establish a family of his own apart from his family of origin.
- Next, he will be "joined" to his wife. God is not talking about *joining* in the sense of "meeting at a party and hooking up at her place afterward." He is referring to a fully devoted lifetime commitment, which suggests "a permanent attraction which transcends genital union."[1]
- Finally, the two will become "one flesh" (NKJV), which means physically intimate, but mentally, emotionally, and spiritually connected as well, as "flesh" refers to mind, body, heart, *and* soul.[2]

Here is the SEV (the Shannon Ethridge Version) translation of this verse: "Grow up, get established, find a suitable mate, get married, and then feel free to have all the sex you want because it is going to bond the two of you together like crazy in every way!"

Think about it. God is the only Mathematician in the universe who can submit an equation such as "One + One = One" and have it be so undeniably true. This one-flesh union is no doubt God's absolute best for us. We humans, though, sometimes have our own ideas of what is best, which are often far cries from what the Creator originally had in mind. We will talk more in question 3 about what can happen when we lean on our own judgment in this area, but for now, let's establish *why* God would place such a boundary around sexuality as to endorse it wholeheartedly in marriage and forbid it in any other relational context.

I think we can best grasp this concept by examining how God designed individuals to best function and how God designed society to best function. Physically, our bodies are simply not designed to have multiple sex partners. Former U.S. Surgeon General C. Everett Koop, MD, emphasized, "When you have sex with someone, you are having sex with everyone they have had sex with for the past ten years, and everyone they and their partners have had sex with for the last ten years."[3] And that is why medical clinic waiting rooms are overflowing with very nervous patients awaiting the results of STD screenings and HIV blood tests. And why so many people wound up on my embalming table in the prime of their lives—in their twenties or early thirties— instead of their eighties or nineties, as it should be. (Yes, I was a mortician for four years before becoming "the sex lady.") We simply cannot deny the fact that multiple sexual partners can wreak havoc on our health.

We also cannot deny that going from sex partner to sex partner wreaks havoc on our mental and emotional health. It is incredibly painful to go through a bitter breakup after having already given yourself to another person sexually. It is like the ultimate rejection. "Yes, you gave me your all . . . but that wasn't good enough. Next person in line, please." *Ouch.* Not what God intended. And when we subject our hearts to this kind of pain over and over, it is like a worn-out strip of Velcro on an old pair of tennis shoes. Over time something that is intended to provide security and safety and protection loses its bonding ability and serves only to leave us vulnerable to exposure and even humiliation.

Think about it. One of the greatest abilities of human beings is our ability to bond tightly with other humans. Take that away and we become empty shells, searching for the next sexual high, with no heart for anyone to hold on to. This is reason enough to protect the sanctity of sex only within a marriage relationship. Yet there is another reason worth mentioning. Spiritually speaking, lovemaking between a committed husband and wife is intended to be the ultimate height of the human experience—not just sexually through an awesome orgasm but also through the enormous spiritual euphoria experienced together. (More on that later.)

Not only is restricting sex to marriage best for individuals, but it is also what keeps society from both imploding (through the decline of moral character) and exploding (through uncontrolled population expansion). It is unfathomable, but let's take a moment to contemplate it as best we can. Let's remove all religious regulations, all emotional sensibilities, all relational ties, all legal boundaries. Let's say humans actually did have free rein to have as much sex with as many people as they want. Marriage means nothing. If the going gets tough, bail out and find another partner. There is no socially acceptable limit to the number of marriages you can rack up. All those children you have brought into the world? They don't really need *both* a mom and a dad, do they? They will figure out a way to make it on the streets while their single parent slaves away at two or three jobs to pay all the bills because the other parent is now paying to help his or her new family survive these tough economic times. Or, better yet, everyone involved in the relational madness and social mayhem can just go on welfare and let the government take care of us. Right?

Of course not. Forgive my sarcasm. I mean no disrespect. I just think it is really important for us to understand just how *stabilizing* it is for a society to embrace the truth that sexual intimacy is incredibly beneficial in the context of marriage, and how, without those appropriate boundaries, there is really nothing distinguishing us from the animal kingdom—meeting, mating, procreating, then repeating as often as the urge strikes. Perhaps this is what God had in mind with panda bears and platypuses and orangutans and octopuses but certainly not with men and women made in His very image.

We must realize that sex is not just about who you get your jollies with. It is about what kind of long-term relationship you are trying to build. It is about what kind of society you want to be a part of. It is about what kind of heritage you want to pass on to future generations that bear your resemblance. It is about what kind of character you hope to construct—both in your own life and in the lives of others.

One last word picture to drive home this point: Think of the difference between a pile of bricks and a brick home. If a tornado rips through a town, that pile of bricks becomes a pile of rubble at best, an arsenal of projectile missiles at worst. But the brick house can actually withstand a pretty severe tornado without a lot of damage. What is the difference? That pile of individual bricks has nothing holding it together, whereas the brick home is literally a fortress of protection.

Think of sex as the mortar that holds a marriage together, that holds a family together, that holds a community together, that holds a society together. If you are reading this book as two single people trying to derive all the benefits of married sex without the marriage license, I hope you will be inspired to seal the deal and build your relationship according to God's perfect blueprint. If you are an engaged couple laying the foundation for a healthy marriage, or if you are a married couple who is trying to discover these spiritual, mental, emotional, and physical passion principles together to strengthen the home you have already built for yourselves, then you are definitely holding the right book.

3. WHAT IF WE WENT TOO FAR SEXUALLY BEFORE WE MARRIED?

Before we go any further, we may need to press the pause button and smooth some feathers that may have been ruffled by the last question. Do most Christians know that God intended sex only for marriage? Most likely. Do humans always live according to that belief? Certainly not. *Rarely* might even be a word I would venture to use. I say that because when I explain to people that my husband was a twenty-six-year-old virgin when we married, they usually respond with, "Wow, that's rare!"

I, however, was part of the estimated 90 percent of people who walk the aisle on their wedding day as a nonvirgin, having head knowledge that premarital sex was wrong, but a heart that was too hungry to ignore the magnetic pull of sexual temptation. And although Greg was determined not to become a part of that club with me, I confess I tried to initiate him anyway. I especially turned up the heat once we bought a house just weeks before our wedding date. I wanted him to move into the house with me or at least stay the night so I wasn't there alone. "Home mortgage papers are more binding than a marriage certificate!" I would insist. My virgin fiancé did not buy into my argument. Although Greg may have been inexperienced, he wasn't ignorant. He knew what would most likely happen if we slept under the same roof. And although I was not getting my way at the time, I have grown so incredibly thankful for his strength of character in those moments.

But not every spouse has that kind of self-control prior to marrying the love of his or her life. And this creates all kinds of interesting dynamics as the years go by. It would be helpful before we get much deeper into this book to examine some of these possible dynamics so that some deep healing can take place and you can focus together on cultivating the passionate sexual relationship you both want in your marriage. (By the way, we will address healing from relationships with past lovers in a future question, but for this section we will stick with what transpired between the two of you before your wedding day.)

Maybe, like me, you are part of the 90 percent club. Perhaps the two of you caved in to sexual temptation at the exact same moment, each taking full responsibility rather than placing any blame on the other. Later, hopefully, you put on your big-girl panties and big-boy boxers, apologized for your own lack of self-control, forgave each other, and moved on. If so, congratulations! Hopefully there is no major harm, no intended foul, no need for any tears or tyranny.

However, many couples report quite a different story:

- Gretchen said, "I told my husband I wanted to be a virgin on my wedding day, but he kept pushing the envelope and pushing my buttons and pushing his luck . . . until he got lucky. At my expense. Rather than recognize what was happening as disrespect and stopping him in his tracks, I eventually gave him what he wanted for fear of losing him if I didn't. Then I felt I *had* to marry him. Otherwise, I'd have been damaged goods. Eighteen years later, I've still not been able to completely forgive him for stealing my dream and making me feel like a hypocrite. Looking at myself in the mirror wearing white on my wedding day made me want to cry."

- Gary wrote in an e-mail, "When I took my wife out on our first date, I had no idea that sex was going to become part of the equation so quickly. I didn't see it coming, and by the time I did, she already had me firing on all cylinders. There was no stopping her or myself at that point. I got so hooked, but I also grew to hate what I'd become—a sex-addicted man who'd abandoned all my moral values. Needless to say, trust and insecurities are *big* issues in our relationship, even after all these years."

- Madeline described her premarital relationship as "addictive in every way. I knew he was mostly a 'father figure' to me, and that I was just balm for his broken soul after a bitter breakup with a previous girlfriend. But that didn't seem to matter to either of us at the time, so we used sex with each other to medicate our emotional pain. Which has only caused even more pain in our marriage. Most days I wish we could rewind the tape and start over with a stronger foundation, but I have no idea how to do that."

- Andrew explained, "Sometimes I feel like the [stereotypical] girl in the relationship because I'm the one willing to 'put out' in order to feel loved and accepted. I've never had a woman simply love me for who I am, rather than what I'm able or willing to do for her sexually. While many guys might love feeling like their wife's 'boy toy,' it makes me feel cheap . . . and nervous that she'll have her head turned by another 'boy toy' in the future."

As these testimonies reveal, premarital sexual activity can do a lot of damage, especially if either spouse feels as if he or she was manipulated or taken advantage of in any way. Professional counseling is often needed to resolve such deeply rooted feelings of betrayal in a relationship. If you suspect that is the case in yours, I encourage you to pursue it. Marriage counseling is, in my opinion, one of the best investments of time, money, and energy a couple can make. However, you could certainly begin the healing process by initiating two small steps that can have a *huge* impact on your relational dynamic:

1. Take responsibility for your part in the dance of sexual dysfunction.
2. Start with a clean slate by forgiving both yourself and your spouse completely.

I once coached a woman who was mourning the loss of her virginity to her persistent husband while they were still dating. While I was trying to show as much compassion as I could, I felt compelled to ask the simple question, "Did he hold a gun to your head?"

She was shocked, but she sat with the question just long enough for something to obviously click in her brain. The hard lines on her face melted as she looked me in the eye and courageously declared, "No. No, he didn't."

I could tell it was a much-needed aha! moment for her, as I thought she might stand up afterward and shout, "Hooray! I don't have to play the victim anymore!" In truth, the responsibility was on *both* their shoulders, not just his. She could have said no just as easily as he could have. We all need to own up to the fact that unless we are truly physically overpowered and forcefully raped, we always have a say in the matter. Perhaps we said no with our words, but our reciprocal and responsive actions probably spoke a lot louder in the heat of the moment. We each must own up to the power that we willingly surrendered at the time, and give up the victim mentality. It serves no good purpose. When we recognize that we weren't victims but, rather, initially-reluctant-yet-ultimately-willing partners, then forgiveness is no longer just a one-way street. It becomes a two-lane highway. It is amazing how much easier it is to forgive another person when we realize how much we ourselves are in need of forgiveness for the exact same infraction. Throwing a stone is not something we are as eager to do when we realize just how much we ourselves belong in the middle of the stone-throwing circle.

If this section has struck a chord in you and/or your spouse, pray the following prayer together.

Lord Jesus, You taught us by example that throwing a stone isn't the way to remedy sin. The blood You shed is the only thing that cleanses us from our past sexual sins, and we thank You for the all-sufficiency of that sacrifice You made on our behalf. Help us to take responsibility for our own actions, forgive ourselves, and extend that same forgiveness to each other. Help us to completely let go of the past so our arms are wide open to embrace the awesome future You have for our marriage bed. Amen.

The *Genesis* of Sex

4. ■ WHAT DOES THE OLD TESTAMENT SAY ABOUT SEX?

IN 2004 WE BEGAN A MASSIVE BUILDING PROJECT TO DOUBLE THE size of an old log cabin, turning it from a little vacation place into what most would consider a dream home. Although we eventually worked with an entire crew of framers, masons, plumbers, electricians, and others, our very first step had to be establishing a relationship with an architect who had a much clearer vision for the project than our simple minds could fathom. Several months and several thousand dollars into that relationship, we had an official set of blueprints that would be referred back to time and time again throughout the building process.

In building our own *marital* dream homes, we may need to do something similar on occasion—reconnect with the Master Architect of marriage and sex, and refer back to *His* blueprints so we can make sure we are following the plan accordingly to build a marriage bed that is solid. That being said, I believe there is no better blueprint to refer back to than the Bible, both the New Testament (which we will dive into in the next sections) and the Old Testament, where we will find God's perfect intentions regarding sexuality, specifically:

- God's original design
- rules and regulations
- honor and integrity
- consequences for compromise
- warnings and wisdom

While you may be incredibly familiar with these teachings already, I hope you will open your mind to some fresh, new revelations as we refer back to the blueprints of healthy sexuality, starting with . . .

GOD'S ORIGINAL DESIGN

In the earliest chapters of Genesis, God created humans in His very own image, breathing life into our lungs and blessings on our masculinity, our femininity, and our relationship to one another. In addition, He also extended a formal invitation to partner with Him in creation, specifically in populating the earth:

> In building our own *marital* dream homes, we may need to do something similar on occasion—reconnect with the Master Architect of marriage and sex, and refer back to *His* blueprints so we can make sure we are following the plan accordingly to build a marriage bed that is solid.

So God created human beings in his image. In the image of God he created them. He created them male and female. God blessed them and said, "Have many children and grow in number." (Genesis 1:27–28 NCV)

Adam had sexual relations with his wife Eve, and she became pregnant. (Genesis 4:1 NCV)

The Old Testament also makes it clear that there is to be absolutely *no* embarrassment, guilt, shame, or inhibition in carrying out God's plan for sexual intimacy in marriage.

The man and his wife were naked, but they were not ashamed. (Genesis 2:25 NCV)

But then sin entered the picture (Genesis 3), and there soon came a need for some specific boundaries to keep humans from hurting themselves and others with their sexual expressions. So being the loving, nurturing, protective God that He is, He gave us a few guidelines.

RULES AND REGULATIONS

In the book of Leviticus, specifically chapters 18, 19, and 20, the Mosaic Law warns us against unhealthy sexual practices, such as:

- Homosexuality—"You must not have sexual relations with a man as you would a woman. That is a hateful sin" (Leviticus 18:22 NCV).
- Bestiality—"You must not have sexual relations with an animal and make yourself unclean with it" (Leviticus 18:23 NCV).
- Prostitution—"Do not dishonor your daughter by making her become a prostitute" (Leviticus 19:29 NCV), and

"No Israelite man or woman must ever become a temple prostitute" (Deuteronomy 23:17 NCV).

- Adultery—"If a man has sexual relations with his neighbor's wife, both the man and the woman are guilty of adultery and must be put to death" (Leviticus 20:10 NCV). (We will talk soon about how, in the Gospels, Jesus revealed a far more effective way of dealing with adultery than killing those involved.)
- Incest—"You must never have sexual relations with your close relatives" (Leviticus 18:6 NCV).

In addition to laying down some necessary laws to guide our sexual behaviors, God also shows us how exercising sexual self-control results in an added measure of His favor.

HONOR AND INTEGRITY

In Genesis 39:6–12 we read the epic story of Joseph, who was sold into slavery by his jealous brothers. He was purchased by Potiphar and soon caught the eye of his master's wife. Handsome Joseph was quite the manly specimen, and Potiphar's wife took notice. Soon she demanded that he sleep with her, a request that could have had some serious consequences if disobeyed. Yet Joseph knew that the consequences of disobeying the Lord would be much greater. So when she cornered him one day, Joseph ran from her at breakneck speed. To cover her own twisted tracks, Potiphar's wife insisted that Joseph tried to rape her, and he was falsely imprisoned as a result. Doesn't sound quite fair, does it? But the story doesn't end there.

After several years of eating humble pie, building spiritual muscles, and ministering to fellow inmates, Joseph interpreted a dream for the king. As a result of his wise interpretation and sage advice, he was not only released from prison but also exalted to one of the most powerful positions in the land—a position from which he was able to save his entire family.

Moral of the story? First, there is *no* shame in running from sexual temptation. Second, while we may suffer some unpleasant consequences for keeping our guard firmly in place, God will certainly be pleased and will eventually honor our choice to live with sexual integrity.

But sadly, not every Old Testament character displayed the same integrity as Joseph.

CONSEQUENCES FOR COMPROMISE

In the eleventh and twelfth chapters of 2 Samuel, we find the story of David, gazing upon a bathing beauty by the name of Bathsheba. Although he learned that she was a married woman, David sent for her anyway and slept with her. Lust gave birth to adultery, and then guess who announced she would be giving birth to David's offspring? Yep, Bathsheba.

David panicked and concocted a scheme to create the illusion that Bathsheba's own husband, Uriah, had impregnated her. But the plan failed miserably when Uriah refused to sleep with his wife while his fellow soldiers were in battle. So David did the unthinkable, sending Uriah to the front lines of that battle to be killed. The adulterer became a murderer.

After Bathsheba had had time to mourn the death of her husband, David brought her to the palace and made her one of his wives, and she gave birth to a son. Problem solved, right? Not exactly. We are told that "the LORD did not like what David had done" (2 Samuel 11:27 NCV).

The prophet Nathan told David a story about a detestable rich man who, although he owned much livestock, stole a little lamb from a poor man. David was outraged and demanded retribution, but felt the sting of rebuke when he realized that the story was really about what he had done to Uriah by stealing his wife. Although the Lord forgave David and allowed him to live, what followed were harsh consequences—a household that rebelled against him, wives who were publicly seduced by other men, and the death of the child who had been conceived by him and Bathsheba. Fortunately, the Lord allowed them to conceive again, and their son, Solomon, was loved by the Lord and became one of the wisest rulers in history, which leads us to a few tidbits of . . .

WARNINGS AND WISDOM

King Solomon wrote the book of Proverbs for "gaining wisdom and instruction; for understanding words of insight; for receiving instruction in prudent behavior, doing what is right and just and fair" (Proverbs 1:2–3 NIV). And a book about wisdom is most certainly not complete without ample warnings against sexual temptation.

Solomon wrote rather graphically about avoiding the clutches of sexual sin:

Why be captivated, my son, by an immoral woman,
or fondle the breasts of a promiscuous woman? . . .

Love wisdom like a sister;
make insight a beloved member of your family.
Let them protect you from an affair with an immoral woman,
from listening to the flattery of a promiscuous woman.

While I was at the window of my house,
  looking through the curtain,
I saw some naive young men,
  and one in particular who lacked common sense.
He was crossing the street near the house of an immoral
  woman,
  strolling down the path by her house.
It was at twilight, in the evening,
  as deep darkness fell.
The woman approached him,
  seductively dressed and sly of heart. . . .

So she seduced him with her pretty speech
  and enticed him with her flattery. . . .

Don't let your hearts stray away toward her.
  Don't wander down her wayward path.
For she has been the ruin of many;
  many men have been her victims.
Her house is the road to the grave.
Her bedroom is the den of death. (Proverbs 5:20; 7:4–10,
  21, 25–27)

The gender could be reversed easily, this passage serving as a warning to women against promiscuous men as well. Both husbands and wives must use wisdom and extreme caution to avoid being seduced sexually. And notice that Solomon's suggested line of defense against such inappropriate entanglements is to *enjoy* a vibrant sexual relationship with the spouse God has given you.

Drink water from your own well—
>   share your love only with your wife.
Why spill the water of your springs in the streets,
>   having sex with just anyone?
You should reserve it for yourselves.
>   Never share it with strangers.

Let your wife be a fountain of blessing for you.
>   Rejoice in the wife of your youth.
She is a loving deer, a graceful doe.
>   Let her breasts satisfy you always.
May you always be captivated by her love. (Proverbs 5:15–19)

Again, this passage applies to women as well, encouraging us to create the perfect love at home rather than searching for it elsewhere. As we look to one another in marriage to satisfy our natural sexual desires, love forms an incredibly strong bond that protects us from Satan's destructive schemes.

The Old Testament has much more to say about sexuality than just the five things highlighted here (especially in the books of Song of Songs and Hosea), so let's continue mining other riches from God's Word, shall we?

5. WHY IS THE SONG OF SOLOMON EVEN IN THE BIBLE?

On a flight from Dallas to Los Angeles, I once found myself seated beside two middle-aged gentlemen who were obviously traveling together and who were each obviously involved in some sort of ministerial role. They debated matters of church politics, doctrine, and Scripture, and my radar went up, of course, when the Song of Solomon came up as a topic of discussion.

The younger man, in the window seat, conjectured, "It's obvious that the Song of Solomon is intended to be strictly a metaphor of God's love for His people."

The older man, in the middle seat, responded firmly, "It's a good theory, but I believe it's more about human passion and earthly marriage. After all, God is not even mentioned in the entire text."

Out of my peripheral vision, I saw the younger man cock one eyebrow, give a *humph!* sound, and turn to stare out the window. After gathering his thoughts, he replied, "Then why would the Song of Solomon even be included in the Bible at all?"

I sat in my aisle seat, awaiting the answer with bated breath, resisting the temptation to turn to the middle man and personally inquire, "Yeah, why *is* it in the Bible if it's more about human passion than God's passion?"

To gain a better understanding of why these writings are in the Bible at all, let's consider what was going on in the culture at the time Song of Songs was written. Neighboring the Israelites (God's chosen people) were the Canaanites, who worshipped their own god, Baal. According to Canaanite beliefs, worshipping Baal guaranteed fertility and prosperity. And a big part of their worship practices included cultic prostitution, where sex between a worshipper and a high priest supposedly guaranteed rain and bountiful crops. If someone refused to participate in such sexual relationships, and crops failed due to drought or pestilence, the sexual stick-in-the-mud was blamed and faced great outrage from the rest of the Canaanites.[1] As a result, there was a lot of pressure to use sex in some very ungodly ways.

So I believe the writer of the Song of Solomon wanted to remind the Israelites of the sanctity of sex within marriage. How? By simply painting a stunningly beautiful portrait of the passion in an *exclusive* love relationship—not one based on cultic prostitution, but one based on commitment, as we see these two lovers so smitten with one another that no one else could possibly turn their heads. It is a celebration of physical and emotional attraction, of overwhelming passion, of all-consuming desire, of verbal affirmation, of sexual expression.

But what has *that* got to do with *God?*

It has *everything* to do with God because God is the Author of all such things.

And I believe that God knew from the beginning of time that sexual passion would be the main topic that would appeal to, distract, occupy, confuse, bewilder, arouse, and fascinate us more so than any other topic. Just look at our movies, music, magazines, and every other form of media under the sun. Sex sells because an insatiable curiosity about sex is the one thing all sexual beings have in common.

As professor of philosophy at Boston College, Peter Kreeft, PhD, says, "There is no subject in the world about which there is more heat and less light. . . . The fact that there are thousands of 'how to do it' books on [sex] does not mean that we know how; in fact, it means the opposite. It is when everybody's pipes are leaking that people buy books on plumbing."[2]

So long before other books were published on the matter, God established His own best-selling whirlwind romance novel through the Song of Solomon. And read through the right lens, neither Harlequin nor *Hustler,* neither *Penthouse* nor *Playboy* can compete.

After multiple readings, I also believe the Song of Solomon

was written as a celebration of not only love, relationship, marriage, and sex but also of how God designed the human body and brain, such that our senses are incredibly heightened under the influence of such passion. Notice how specific things are mentioned throughout the chapters that appeal to all five of our senses:

- Taste—kisses like fine wine, lover like an apple tree, lips like honeycomb, and milk and honey under the tongue
- Smell—exquisite perfumes, sachets of myrrh between the breasts, clusters of henna blossoms, fragrance of blossoming vines, incense from fine spices
- Hearing—seasons of singing, cooing of doves, sweetness of a lover's voice, a garden fountain, a well of flowing water, a lover knocking at the door
- Feeling—a verdant bed; a lover's embrace; longing for the sights, sounds, and feel of her lover; a stolen heart due to a glance; a locked garden, an enclosed spring, a sealed fountain; a pounding heart at her lover's arrival; a sunken heart at her lover's absence; feeling faint with love; unquenchable desire
- Sight—a wide variety of physical attributes—from facial features to intimate body parts—are likened to such awe-inspiring things as a harnessed mare, a scarlet ribbon, pomegranate halves, strings of jewels, gold, silver, polished ivory, sapphires, marble, doves, lilies among thorns, gazelles, flocks of goats and sheep, the fairness of the moon, the brightness of the sun, the majesty of the stars

When the Song of Solomon so fervently and unashamedly describes the lover's kiss, as well as the woman's navel as a goblet

CELEBRATE THE SPIRITUAL SIDE OF SEX

of fine wine (Song of Songs 1:2, 7:2), and her stature as "like a palm tree," and her "breasts . . . like its clusters of fruit," such that her lover declares, "I will climb the palm tree and take hold of its fruit" (7:7–8), the reader certainly gets the idea that God is *not* modest when it comes to committed love and sexual passion within marriage.

So why in the world should our perspective on sex and marriage be any different? It shouldn't be. So while other religions may use group sex or cultic prostitution to invoke their impotent gods, we can best worship our omnipotent God through celebrating our sexuality (and all of the sensory-pleasing activities that come along with it) through an exclusive, passionate relationship with our own personal lovers, our spouses.

PONDER THE PRINCIPLE

- ⚘ Which of your senses is most delightfully engaged as you are making love to your spouse? Your sense of sight, smell, hearing, taste, or touch?
- ⚘ Do you believe God intended for married couples to enjoy such a sensory extravaganza when He created sexual intimacy? Why or why not?
- ⚘ Next time you make love, take a moment to consider each of your senses. Look not just at the body but also into the eyes of your partner. Notice how your spouse smells and tastes, listen to the heartbeat, the breathing, and the voice as the two of you interact. Delight in the skin-to-skin contact. Consider how consciously doing this might inspire a deeper level of worship and gratitude toward the Creator of our sexuality.

32

6. WHY DID GOD TELL HOSEA TO MARRY A PROSTITUTE?

I frequently joke about how women are told by well-intentioned parents to marry a doctor or a lawyer, but I have always said, "Marry a financial manager." With a husband who is a certified public accountant, I have not had to file a tax return in over two decades, and I wouldn't have to balance a checkbook at all, except that I am too much of a control freak not to do so.

Parents also give their sons similar advice, such as, "Marry a good cook," or "Marry a girl from a nice family." Not that this is any guarantee of gourmet meals or civil in-laws, but it is sage advice. But can you imagine parents telling their sons, "Marry a prostitute"?

Absurd, right? Yet that is exactly what God did when He spoke to the prophet Hosea. We read in Hosea 1:2 that the Lord said to Hosea, "Go and marry a prostitute, so that some of her children will be conceived in prostitution. This will illustrate how Israel has acted like a prostitute by turning against the LORD and worshiping other gods."

Scholars differ in their opinions about whether Hosea's wife, Gomer, was actually a prostitute when Hosea married her, but the more popular opinion is that she most likely became one *after* her marriage to Hosea. Why? This entire story is a reflection of God's love relationship with His own people, brought to life in a most bizarre but, ultimately, beautiful way.

As a reminder of the big picture leading up to this point in history, here is a quick recap.

- God called Abraham into a new land and established an everlasting covenant with him, saying:

"I will make you into a great nation. I will bless you and make you famous, and you will be a blessing to others. I will bless those who bless you and curse those who treat you with contempt. All the families on earth will be blessed through you." (Genesis 12:2–3)

This covenant would bind all of Abraham and Sarah's descendants to God in a special way, from their son, Isaac, their grandson Jacob, and their great-grandson Joseph (whom we discussed in question 4), all the way up to the birth of Jesus many generations later. The people of Israel were raised knowing that the almighty God was their Divine Guide.

- Due to a severe famine, the Israelites became slaves in Egypt. But true to the covenant He had made with these "chosen people," God eventually led them out of Egyptian slavery through some pretty miraculous events—the dramatic ten plagues, when Pharaoh refused to set God's people free; the angel of death killing every Egyptian firstborn yet "passing over" the houses of the Israelites; the successful plundering of the Egyptians on the Israelites' way out of town; the parting of the Red Sea; and the drowning of those Egyptian soldiers in hot pursuit of them. God was indeed their Divine Deliverer.

- As they wandered in the desert, God gave Moses a set of laws for the people to live by and govern themselves by so they could live as holy and happy people. He provided for them daily during their forty years of wandering in the desert, quenching their thirst with water gushing from rocks, raining down manna and quail from heaven, and keeping their clothes and sandals from ever wearing out in spite of all those miles of traveling. He ultimately led them to a fertile "Promised Land" piece of real estate. He was their Divine Provider.

But you also might recall that this special group of people had a proclivity toward idol worship, as first seen when Moses came down from Mount Sinai with the Ten Commandments only to discover that his brother, Aaron, had succumbed to the people's request for a golden calf to worship. They grew tired of waiting on Moses' God and decided to settle for crafting their own. Big mistake.

And at the writing of the book of Hosea, history is obviously repeating itself, as it often does in dysfunctional families. Through many generations, changes of leadership, and bloody battles, especially the one against the king of Syria, the strength of Israel's army had dwindled to next to nothing—fifty horsemen, ten chariots, and ten thousand foot soldiers (2 Kings 13:7). But through the leadership of Jehoash and Jeroboam, Israel had regained her strength, and they now enjoyed a time of economic prosperity and great wealth (2 Kings 13:25; 2 Chronicles 26:10). They were feeling quite proud of themselves—so proud, in fact, that they took a bow . . . in the direction of Baal and a few Asherah poles. Somehow, worshipping false gods still tickled their fancy, but that certainly did not tickle God. So He sent the prophet Hosea to preach, or rather to live out, the following three-point sermon:

1. God is faithful and compassionate, in spite of our repeated unfaithfulness.

"When Israel was a child, I loved him, and out of Egypt I called my son. But the more they were called, the more they went away from me. They sacrificed to the Baals and they burned incense to images. . . . My people are determined to turn from me. . . . My heart is changed within me; all my compassion is aroused. I will not carry out my fierce anger, nor will I devastate Ephraim again. For I am God, and not a man—the Holy One among you. I will not come against their cities." (Hosea 11:1–2, 7, 8–9 NIV)

2. God's intense love prompts disciplinary measures for our unfaithfulness.

"I will punish her for the days she burned incense to the Baals; she decked herself with rings and jewelry, and went after her lovers, but me she forgot," declares the LORD. (Hosea 2:13 NIV)

3. When we repent of our unfaithfulness, we will be forgiven and blessed.

"Therefore I am now going to allure her; I will lead her into the wilderness and speak tenderly to her. There I will give her back her vineyards, and will make the Valley of Achor a door of hope. There she will respond as in the days of her youth, as in the day she came up out of Egypt. In that day," declares the LORD, "you will call me 'my husband'; you will no longer call me 'my master.' . . . I will betroth you to me forever; I will betroth you in righteousness and justice, in love and compassion. I will betroth you in faithfulness, and you will acknowledge the Lord." (Hosea 2:14–16, 19–20 NIV)

If you have never read the short book of Hosea (only fourteen chapters long) as a couple, I encourage you to do so. It is truly one of the most graphic yet gripping stories ever told, as well as one of the most vivid pictures of the absolutely committed covenant relationship that God extends to His people. And this same dynamic still exists today. Even when we are unfaithful toward God, He remains steadfast in His faithfulness toward us.

It is hard enough to imagine having that kind of irrevocable relationship extended to us from the Maker of the universe, but let's strain our brains a little more. Could you also imagine what marriage could be like if we tried to love *each other* like that? How over-the-top passionate our passionate moments could become if we were absolutely, positively, totally secure—both in our marriages and in our marriage beds?

Seriously, what if everyone consistently viewed marriage as a forever-binding relationship—no escape hatch, no eject button, no loophole to crawl out of? What if your spouse literally said to you, "I'm not going anywhere, *no matter what!*"? What if *you* were committed enough to declare that yourself?

I was the recipient of such extravagant love only a few years into our marriage. We had had a big knock-down-drag-out discussion about some ridiculous something that simply eludes us

> The short book of Hosea . . . is truly one of the most graphic yet gripping stories ever told . . . Even when we are unfaithful toward God, He remains steadfast in His faithfulness toward us.

now, and being the less mature one in the marriage, I was preparing to storm out the door and drive to my parents' house. I went to put my shoes on and grab my favorite pillow, but by the time I came back to the front door, Greg was literally sprawled out across the threshold of the locked door, all six feet, seven inches of him. He tearfully declared, "No one is leaving this house! Divorce is not an option, so let's just figure this out because I'm not going anywhere, and neither are you!"

While some women may have taken this as a challenge and stepped right over him on their way out the door, I melted. Even though choking down humble pie wasn't my idea of the perfect evening, I loved the fact that Greg was being the spiritual leader who was willing to iron the wrinkles out of our relationship, even if he had to take a lot of heat to make that happen. We talked into the wee hours of the night and woke up the next day totally in love again, more in love than before that argument had occurred. To channel all of that relational commitment, forgiveness, and unconditional love into tender lovemaking was the most natural thing in the world.

Marriage is intended to be more than just a piecrust promise— you know, *easily made, easily broken*. It is designed to be a covenant relationship—one that withstands the test of time, the test of all sorts of trials and tribulations. Every marriage that has ever gone the distance has had that covenant tested—most likely many times, if the truth be told. So regardless of our idiosyncrasies or insecurities . . . in spite of personality differences or parenting styles . . . regardless of money management issues or sexual struggles . . . are you willing to cut the umbilical cord from your own family of origin? To erase the bread-crumb trail back toward independence? Are you willing to put *all* your emotional eggs in

THE *GENESIS* OF SEX

this basket and declare to one another, "Neither of us is going any-where, especially not me!" so that you can both exhale and know that regardless of the storms that swell, you are safe in each other's presence?

If so, consider praying together the prayer that follows.

Lord, thank You for how You have proven Yourself to be such a faithful God, in spite of the fact that faithfulness is not the strong suit of Your people. We are so easily distracted from You and so easily distracted from the roles You call us to as husband and wife. But God, we don't want a temporary marriage that folds like a house of cards under pressure. We want to love each other the way You love us—unconditionally, unreservedly, without holding the past over each other's head or using our weaknesses as weapons against each other. So we place our marriage in Your hands, Lord, knowing that only You can protect us and provide the spiritual insight that we need to truly embrace and celebrate the precious relationship we share. In Jesus' name, amen.

The Gospel Truth

7. WHAT DID JESUS SAY ABOUT SEX? AND HOW CAN HE POSSIBLY RELATE TO OUR STRUGGLES?

SOME OF MY FAVORITE QUESTIONS TO POSE TO AN AUDIENCE when I am speaking are: "Was Jesus tempted sexually?" and "Did He ever have sexual thoughts and feelings?"

I usually give the audience several minutes to discuss this question, and then I ask for folks to shout out their conclusions. On occasion someone will respond, "No. Jesus wasn't tempted sexually because He was God." And then I will see lots of heads turning from side to side, responding negatively as if they do not agree. Of course, they are not denying that Jesus was God. But they also know that Jesus was *both* fully God *and* fully man. In John 1:14 we read, "So the Word [God] became human and made his home among us." Or as Eugene Peterson puts it in *The Message*, "The Word became flesh and blood, and moved into the neighborhood."

But more often the response I receive to the question about whether Jesus was ever tempted sexually is a wholehearted, "*Yes!* Jesus *did* have sexual thoughts and feelings." And many are even able to back their theory up with the following passage of

Scripture: "This High Priest of ours understands our weaknesses, for he faced all of the same testings we do, yet he did not sin" (Hebrews 4:15).

Did you catch that? He faced *all* of our same testings. There is no asterisk with a disclaimer at the bottom of the page that says, "Except sexually. Jesus wasn't *that* kind of guy." No, in fact, Jesus *was* tempted in *every way* known to man (and woman), yet He showed us by example that we don't have to give in to those feelings and live outside of God's perfect will for our lives and relationships.

Something that has really stood out to me as I have pondered this passage is that Jesus did not avoid sin because He *wasn't tempted at all*—He avoided sin *even though* He was tempted! This is a very important distinction to make. There is a big difference between not sinning when you are tempted and not sinning because you are not tempted at all. For example, it doesn't take much for me to avoid alcohol because I simply don't like the taste. But my husband enjoys a nice cold beer when we go to certain restaurants, so for him to exercise self-control after one beer is a lot more impressive than for me to exercise self-control in the same scenario. (I do, however, know the temporary intoxication of toxic relationships. Funny how those two words, *intoxication* and *toxic*, are so similar. So that is where my self-control is occasionally tested.)

Perhaps you are thinking, *What's that got to do with Jesus? I don't think Jesus was tempted by that kind of stuff.*

Really? You don't think He enjoyed the exquisite taste of that ordinary water He turned into the finest wine?

So now you may be thinking, *Well, okay, it was impressive that Jesus always knew when to stop drinking. But surely Jesus wasn't tempted by inappropriate relationships.*

Again, *really?*

Think about it. Jesus had beautiful women following Him from town to town, spending their own money to care for His personal needs, washing His feet with their tears and drying them with their long silky hair, anointing His body with expensive perfumes, and so on. I am sure that many of these women were enamored with Jesus' strength of character, authority, compassion, and verbal talents (talk about meeting a woman's emotional needs!), not to mention His amazing miracles of healing and restoration. Let's not be naive. Jesus could have easily used one of these women for a little ego stroke of His own, and no one would have even noticed. But Jesus kept His ego very much in check. Even as the Son of God (which was far more impressive in crowds than being Elvis or the Beatles, when you think about it), Jesus wasn't interested in what He could get for Himself while on this earth, but rather, what He could give to us. And one of the greatest things He gave to us, besides eternal salvation through the personal sacrifice He made on the cross, was an amazing example of what it looks like to be tempted in every way, yet without sin.

So in answer to the question, "How can Jesus possibly understand our sexual struggles?" I say, "Hello? He has walked in our shoes. He has experienced our thoughts. He has felt our feelings." And I love how the following verse, Hebrews 4:16, encourages us: "So let us come boldly to the throne of our gracious God. There we will receive his mercy, and we will find grace to help us when we need it most." Therefore, there is no one more qualified to coach us through our most tempting moments than Jesus Himself.

Before we move on to some other things that Jesus taught us about sexual issues, I want to highlight the fact that He showed us by example that the sexual thoughts and feelings we all have are *not* sinful.

How do I know? If Jesus had sexual thoughts and feelings and yet was "without sin," then how can those be sin? It's an impossible equation! No, it's what we choose to *do* with those sexual thoughts and feelings that makes all the difference between holiness (the pursuit of God's pleasure) and hedonism (the pursuit of our own pleasure).

In addition to being a living, breathing example of sexual integrity, Jesus also had a few interesting things to say about sexual sin, particularly in the Sermon on the Mount, where He made the following strong statements:

- "You have heard the commandment that says, 'You must not commit adultery.' But I say, anyone who even looks at a woman with lust has already committed adultery with her in his heart." (Matthew 5:27–28)
- "So if your eye—even your good eye—causes you to lust, gouge it out and throw it away. It is better for you to lose one part of your body than for your whole body to be thrown into hell. And if your hand—even your stronger hand—causes you to sin, cut it off and throw it away. It is better for you to lose one part of your body than for your whole body to be thrown into hell." (Matthew 5:29–30)
- "You have heard the law that says, 'A man can divorce his wife by merely giving her a written notice of divorce.' But I say that a man who divorces his wife, unless she has been unfaithful, causes her to commit adultery. And anyone who marries a divorced woman also commits adultery." (Matthew 5:31–32)

These passages can sound like bitter pills to swallow. Most of us would be walking around blind and castrated if we took these passages literally. In fact, I was shocked and disheartened to learn of a woman who, as a result of her misinterpreting these passages, gouged out her own eye. How sad that she didn't understand God's grace to be sufficient, or His mercies to be new to her every morning as He promises (2 Corinthians 12:9, Lamentations 3:22–23).

I am not saying that Jesus wasn't being serious in these verses; I am simply saying that He was using extreme language to convey just how seriously He wants us to treat the sanctity of not just our bodies but also our hearts and minds, as well as our marriage relationships. To loosely paraphrase (using the SEV again), these passages might be interpreted accordingly:

- When you notice a beautiful person, give credit to the Creator, not the creation. Don't go out of your way to try to make that person yours if he or she (or you) belongs to someone else. Show some respect, both for the other person and for yourself. Take your mental and emotional integrity as seriously as you take your sexual integrity.
- Never assume that until you have sex with another person, there is no harm in looking and leering. Those inappropriately obsessive thoughts and sexually stirring stares will lead you exactly where you know you should not go, so guard your eyes, heart, and mind just as vigilantly as you guard your body.
- Divorce is not the answer for every marital woe. Husband and wife belong to one another forever, so take your wedding vows seriously and be faithful to each other. Don't just hop

from one marriage relationship to another. Instead, figure out how to make it work and make love last.

If we stopped reading at Matthew 5, it would be easy to assume that Jesus has little compassion for the sexual and emotional temptations we face. But let's consider two other stories included in the Gospels that prove this to be a false assumption.

THE WOMAN AT THE WELL

In John 4, we read about Jesus' encounter with a Samaritan woman who was drawing water from a well. He asked her for a drink, and she was shocked that a Jewish man was willing to speak to a Samaritan (in their day, this equated to the lofty elite rubbing elbows with the lowly poor).

In addition to asking for a drink, Jesus offered her insight on how to find "living water," a metaphor for a satisfying intimate relationship with Him. As the exchange continued, we learn that she had broken all the rules about marriage and sexual integrity . . . several times. She had had five husbands and was currently living with a man who wasn't her husband at all.

So what did Jesus do? Did He reject her? Walk away with His nose in the air, eager to find someone more worthy of this gift of living water? No. He went out of His way to shed some light into her life, explaining how to find the fulfillment she was searching for. He looked beyond her weaknesses, acknowledged her needs, and revealed Himself as the only One who could fully and eternally quench her thirsty soul. As a result of this encounter, the Samaritan woman returned to her home and set everyone's hearts ablaze for Jesus upon hearing her testimony.

Yes, even the most broken people can become beautiful

vessels for God's lavish love to be poured out upon others. And speaking of broken people, let's take a look at another example of how Jesus treated the sexually broken . . .

THE WOMAN CAUGHT IN ADULTERY

In John 8 we discover a desperate woman who was in a lot of hot water. She had been found in bed with a man, and that man was not her husband. While the story does not include how the legalistic Pharisees dealt with the man involved, they were ready to stone the woman to death, as the Old Testament law of Moses allowed. But they used this situation to test Jesus. They asked Him, "What do *You* say we should do?"

Did Jesus preach a hellfire-and-brimstone sermon about adultery? Demand that body parts be mutilated to prevent a recurring episode? No. Jesus showed us a higher law to live by—the law of love and mercy. Rather than wagging a finger in her face, Jesus stooped down and used that finger to write in the sand. No one knows what He wrote, but perhaps it was the names of the other men in the crowd she had slept with. That would have caused them to drop their rocks, for sure. Or perhaps He was just tracing patterns and giving them a chance to cool off. The Pharisees continued to press Him for an answer, so He brilliantly declared, "Anyone here who has never sinned can throw the first stone at her" (John 8:7 NCV).

Silence. Then I imagine the sound of rocks dropping to the ground, one after another, given up in defeat rather than hurled in disgust.

There was no condemnation to be dished out that day. Only compassion and gentle conviction. "You may go now, but don't sin anymore," Jesus lovingly said to her (John 8:11 NCV) and sent her on her way. The one sinless man in the crowd, the One who could have justifiably thrown a stone, chose not to.

So how can we read these true stories and believe that Jesus cannot possibly relate to our sexual struggles? That He would never understand what it is like to be a sexual human being? He can, and He does. He has been there. And He is there with us each time we are there too.

8. WHY IS THE RELATIONSHIP BETWEEN JESUS AND HIS CHURCH DESCRIBED AS A BRIDEGROOM/BRIDE RELATIONSHIP?

Throughout Scripture we see many word pictures describing the relationship that God has, or wants to have, with His people. For example, we see God as a skillful Potter, Daily Bread, and Living Water . . . a special Friend and a doting Father . . . a protective Shepherd . . . a Sovereign King . . . a Merciful Savior.

But perhaps you have also recognized how often in Scripture Jesus is referred to as a Bridegroom and how the church is called "His bride" and wondered, as I did many times, *What's up with that?*

So I actually set aside a year of study on this very topic, combing the Bible from the first book of Genesis to the last book of Revelation. I also researched ancient Jewish wedding traditions to see how they might parallel what we read (but rarely fully comprehend) in Scripture. And to say that I was surprised by all that I learned is a huge understatement. It actually rocked my world and continues to do so on a daily basis. Suddenly God was no longer a distant disciplinarian but the Lover of my Soul, who could satisfy me far more than any human, including my spouse, ever could.

This knowledge helped me take the burden of responsibility off my husband's shoulders to be my all-in-all. Instead, I am learning to simply love him for who he is and to experience a level of passion in my relationship with God that has sustained me and fed me the way blood feeds muscle.

Although I have written a book about those epiphanies, called *Completely His: Loving Jesus Without Limits*,[1] I want to encapsulate a few of my findings here because I think they provide great insight into the type of relationship God longs to have with us and how He used the analogy of marriage to communicate His passionate pursuit of us.

> By offering the cup, Jesus was asking His disciples (and us) to be His spiritual bride.

As I began my search, I wondered about the origin of some of our Christian traditions, thinking, perhaps, I had missed some cryptic connections to this picture of intimacy that a bridegroom and bride share. Indeed, there are many things.

- Communion—This public display of affection wasn't just Jesus offering bread and wine as a symbol of His body, which would be broken for the remission of our sins. In Jewish custom a man who wanted to propose marriage to his beloved poured a cup of wine and offered it to her to drink. She could refuse the cup, thereby refusing his proposal, or she could drink from the cup, in essence saying, "I accept your offer." So by offering the cup, Jesus was asking His disciples (and us) to be His spiritual bride:

  After supper he took another cup of wine and said, "This cup is the new covenant between God and his people—an agreement confirmed with my blood, which is poured out as a sacrifice for you." (Luke 22:20)

- Baptism—This public display of repentance wasn't just John the Baptist dunking people in water as a sign of their belief in the coming Messiah, as if they were joining a holy rollers club or something. A betrothed Jewish woman, in preparation for her wedding day, goes through a ceremonial cleansing in a *mikvah*, where she is fully immersed in a body of "living water" in anticipation of her groom's return for her. By being baptized we are declaring our belief that our heavenly Bridegroom is returning for us as well, and we are allowing the Holy Spirit to prepare us as Christ's pure and spotless bride.

"You yourselves know how plainly I [John the Baptist] told you, 'I am not the Messiah. I am only here to prepare the way for him.' It is the bridegroom who marries the bride, and the best man is simply glad to stand with him and hear his vows. Therefore, I am filled with joy at his success." (John 3:28–29)

- Crucifixion—The blood that Jesus shed was a necessary sacrifice to cleanse us of the sin that separates us from God, but it also served another purpose—to satisfy the "bride price" for you and me and every other Christ-follower who ever lived. Whenever a young man wanted to marry a woman, he had to negotiate a bride price that would be paid to her father for her hand in marriage as a sign that he was serious about taking care of her. The bride price for all of humanity was exorbitantly high, but our Bridegroom paid it with His very life. We belong completely to Him!

[Jesus] told [Peter, James, and John], "My soul is crushed with grief to the point of death. Stay here and keep watch with me." He went on a little farther and bowed with his face to the ground, praying, "My Father! If it is possible, let this cup of suffering be taken away from me. Yet I want your will to be done, not mine." (Matthew 26:38–39)

- Heaven—We may wonder why Jesus cannot still be here in the flesh, as it would be much easier to believe in Him if we could just see Him. But according to Jewish tradition, a bridegroom who proposes marriage to his bride must leave her, return to his father's home, and build on an adjoining room—a bridal chamber—where their love will eventually be consummated after the wedding. The only one who can pronounce that the room construction is complete is the father, so we can be assured that Jesus is simply awaiting God's green light to return for His beloved bride—that's *us*! *Woohoo!*

"There is more than enough room in my Father's home. If this were not so, would I have told you that I am going to prepare a place for you? When everything is ready, I will come and get you, so that you will always be with me where I am." (John 14:2–3)

- The Wedding Feast of the Lamb—When Jesus returns for us, as promised in Scripture, He is not returning merely as a Master, Savior, or Friend. No. The book of Revelation tells us how this magnificent, epic story will end: Christ will return to earth as a heavenly Bridegroom, and there will be a grand and glorious wedding feast that will impress even Martha Stewart and Oprah Winfrey. And you and I are invited to that wedding feast, not just as guests but as the bride!

"Let us be glad and rejoice,
     and let us give honor to him.
For the time has come for the wedding feast of the Lamb,
     and his bride has prepared herself.
She has been given the finest of pure white linen to wear."
     For the fine linen represents the good deeds of
     God's holy people.

And the angel said to me, "Write this: Blessed are those who are invited to the wedding feast of the Lamb." And he added, "These are true words that come from God." (Revelation 19:7–9)

God has been wooing and pursuing His people since the beginning of time, and now we have the most highly anticipated event in history to look forward to—the return of Jesus as our heavenly Bridegroom. And we will be able to bask in His glorious presence throughout eternity.

In the meantime, here is our challenge: our earthly marriages should reflect the same passion that Christ possesses for His bride, the church. The apostle Paul explains this correlation clearly in Ephesians 5:31–32:

As the Scriptures say, "A man leaves his father and mother and is joined to his wife, and the two are united into one." This is a great mystery, but it is an illustration of the way Christ and the church are one.

Did you catch that? Husbands and wives are considered as permanently bonded and forever united as Jesus is to the church. Do we have this level of commitment in our marriages? Or more personally, do *you* have this level of commitment in *your* marriage?

Oh, but marriage is hard! you may be thinking.

I know! Anyone who has been married any length of time will most likely echo that sentiment. But let's remember that although we typically think of the word *passion* being defined as "ardent affection" or "sexual desire," there is a whole lot more to it. Even Webster's Dictionary is smart enough to list the primary definition of *passion* as "the sufferings of Christ between the night of the Last Supper and his death."[2]

We may have to suffer for the sake of marriage at times, but let's face it. None of us has had to suffer nearly to the degree that our heavenly Bridegroom has already suffered for us. So let's pause to lift our hearts in praise.

Dearest Lord Jesus, You have set such an amazing example of sacrificial love. Leaving heaven to come to earth so that You could draw us unto You is the most remarkable and romantic thing anyone has ever done—period! Regardless of our unfaithfulness, You have given Your very life to redeem and restore us into right relationship with You, and we give You thanks and praise for loving us so perfectly and so completely. Please bless us with an extraordinary ability to show such unconditional passion and commitment to our spouses, and help our marriages serve the world as a clear reflection of Your lavish love for us. Amen.

9. WHAT IS THE CONNECTION BETWEEN SEXUALITY AND SPIRITUALITY?

No words in the English language could possibly describe the look of panic on my mom's face as she pulled into the driveway to witness me standing barefoot in the dew-covered grass, holding a fallen electrical line in my hand. I had been watching *Sesame Street*, when suddenly the TV went totally dead, along with all the lights in the house. I went outside to ask my dad to investigate, but stumbled upon a potential explanation when I saw the severed black cord lying limp on the front lawn. So I picked it up, as if somehow I could reconnect it to its power source and restore everything to the way it was supposed to be. And, amazingly, I lived to tell about it.

In many ways this section of the book is my attempt to do the same thing—to reconnect married couples to their Power Source and to restore passion and freedom in the marriage bed. Hopefully I will get better results this time and avoid any shocked facial expressions in the process.

Asking the question, "Is there any connection between sexuality and spirituality?" is the equivalent of asking, "Is there any connection between body and spirit?"

Think of the spirit as the "energy" we are given as humans who are made in the image of God. Think of our body as the conduit through which that energy flows. Without the conduit (the body), there would be no way for us to experience that energy and let it flow from ourselves to another human being. But without the energy (the spirit), our bodies alone cannot muster the human connection we naturally crave. Oh, many try. They find human outlets for their physical sexual desires—manipulative seduction, child molestation, sexual abuse, sexual addiction, prostitution, human trafficking—it wears all kinds of ugly masks.

But a physical connection to someone with whom we also share a strong spiritual and emotional bond, that is something else entirely. That is pure love . . . romance . . . passion . . . intimacy . . . ecstasy . . . euphoria.

When you are expressing your sexuality in the way our Designer intended, there is an enormous, undeniable connection between sexuality and spirituality. Humans are sexual. Humans are spiritual. It is the primary common denominator among us all. Are there spiritual people who are not sexual? No. Absolutely not. There are spiritual people who aren't *sexually active*, such as priests, monks, or nuns who have pledged themselves to a lifestyle of celibacy, or single people who are purposely holding out for marriage. But they are still sexual beings and will be until they die.

Are there sexual people who are not spiritual? That depends on whom you ask. Some would say that those who do not have a relationship with Jesus are not spiritual. This may be an acceptable definition of Christianity, but is a very narrow definition of spirituality. Others would say that *all* people are spiritual, simply by the fact that they are alive, regardless of whether they are currently practicing any sort of spiritual activities or disciplines. I agree with this latter camp. We all are made in the image of God, whether we acknowledge it or not, whether we acknowledge God or not.

You simply cannot take the spirit out of the body (at least not until that body is dead). Just as you cannot separate two sides of the same coin. Nor can you take the protein out of a Black Angus steak. Or take the chocolate out of a chocolate bunny, as my friend Steve Holladay says.

It is all swirled together, sexuality and spirituality, never to be separated. So since we cannot possibly separate the body and spirit, or sexuality and spirituality, how about looking to see what we can learn from fully integrating and celebrating the synergy between the two?

In *The Intimate Connection: Male Sexuality, Masculine Spirituality*, author James B. Nelson reveals that our longing for one another is really a longing for God. He explains:

> We are yearning for closer, more fulfilling, more life-giving connectedness with others, with our world, and with ourselves. This means we are yearning for closer connectedness with God, the heart of the universe itself. When we yearn for life-giving relationships with any person or part of creation, we are at the very same time reaching for God. For, according to an incarnationalist faith, God is the spiritual presence who becomes incarnate in and through creaturely flesh. Another way of saying this is that we are simply longing for more life-giving connectedness between our sexuality and our spirituality.[3]

Perhaps this is a new way of thinking for you—that God "becomes incarnate in and through our own flesh." Although

Christians are taught to loathe "the flesh," let's remember that the Son of God became flesh Himself (John 1:14 and Hebrews 2:14). Scholars believe that when the Bible warns against "the flesh," it's referring to our fallen sinful nature, not our bodily desires.[4]

In addition the Bible tells us in Ephesians 6:12: "For we are not fighting against flesh-and-blood enemies [not even our own flesh and blood], but against evil rulers and authorities of the unseen world, against mighty powers in this dark world, and against evil spirits in the heavenly places." In every battle we face the best strategy is to first "define the enemy." Well, Christian brothers and sisters, the enemy is *not* our sexuality. It is *not* our physical cravings. These are all God-given desires because our bodies are, in fact, temples of the Holy Spirit (1 Corinthians 6:19). So perhaps instead of viewing our flesh as this evil thing that is to be despised and derided, we can learn to celebrate our bodies as the conduit through which God's Spirit flows, as well as the conduit through which sexual energy flows toward one another. Indeed, our bodies and the sexual energy flowing through them are nothing short of sacred.

Charles Henderson has reinforced the notion that our sexuality and spirituality are irrevocably intertwined:

The original unity of flesh and spirit, God and humankind, is replaced by a tragic polarity. Not only are human beings now at war with each other, but mind and body are divided against themselves . . .

Jesus identified the corrupt religious leaders of his day and time as being more responsible for humanity's moral problems [than the prostitutes and sinners], for the self-appointed guardians of goodness and truth defined sex as evil and thus made sinners of us all. Jesus saw that self-righteous piety is equally dangerous as promiscuity, for both these attitudes intensify the antagonism between flesh and spirit.

Today the same problem is before us. Whenever sexuality and spirituality are regarded as separate and unrelated things, then both dimensions suffer. For sex is demeaning when it is reduced to the level of a commodity, and religion is demeaning when it is a matter of dry ritual or abstract doctrine.[5]

When you pause to really ponder it, you have to admit it is quite fascinating that God would create us in His image *and* as sexual beings, simultaneously! It is easy to wonder, *But* why *did God make us this way?*

Quite frankly, I believe it is so that we can know Him, experience Him, and fall in love with Him all the more. As distantly as several years ago and as recently as just in the past few days, I have been contemplating this very question. I think I could meditate on it for a hundred years and still not come up with all the answers. But here is just a smattering of my thoughts on what God shows me about Himself through the avenue of my sexuality:

- A coaching client once asked me, "Why did God create us in such a way that we have physiological responses to our emotions? When I'm attracted to someone, why do I get butterflies in my stomach, sweaty palms, and a racing heart? Why do I get all giddy?" At first I responded, "I have no idea," but then it was as if God opened up my brain and poured the answer in, like liquid Drano to unclog my thoughts.

He said, *Shannon, I created humans to respond to love like that so they'd know how I feel when they turn their hearts and attentions toward Me!*

I sat there, blown away for a few seconds. When I shared the epiphany with my coaching client, she was blown away too. *The God of the universe gets giddy over us when we turn toward Him?* Yes, He does. And He has given you a glimpse into that fact through the thoughts and feelings you have had toward the object of your affections (your spouse).

- One lazy Saturday morning I was longing for my husband to get out of the shower and come back to bed. For a moment I wondered, *Why does my body literally* long *to have him inside of me?* And it was as if God was just waiting for me to ask, as the answer immediately came: *Just as a woman longs to have her husband inside her, I long to be inside My bride,* God said, very matter-of-factly. *The main difference is that a human husband can penetrate only so deeply, but My Holy Spirit penetrates every nerve and fiber of the soul.*

- One day I was contemplating why God designed the human body to feel such intense pleasure when we experience orgasm. (If you haven't crossed this bridge in your marriage yet, I'll have some helpful tips for you in the last section of the book. I promise!) Seriously, sex feels plenty good while it is happening, and it creates beautiful babies, and it bonds a couple together in extraordinary ways, so why give us such a stunningly ripe cherry on top as *orgasm?* God's reply to the question? Just like a fun game of peekaboo, our heavenly Father wanted to give us just a glimpse of what we have to look forward to—the big finale, if you will. Is there any moment in our existence in which we feel a more primordial delight, a greater loss of control (in a good way), or a greater sense of absolute euphoria than in those sacred moments of extreme, intense pleasure? I cannot help but believe that when Christ returns for us someday and ushers us into our heavenly home, the intensity of that pleasure is going to be even more mind-blowing and soul stirring than the most amazing orgasmic experience we have ever had.

So if there is such a powerful connection between our sexuality and our spirituality, perhaps investing a little more spiritual energy in preparing for sexual encounters is a wise move.

Would you like to guess what we have found to be the *best* aphrodisiac available? Prayer! When we snuggle up together and hold each other in our arms, then pour out our hearts to God on behalf of one another, it creates such an intense bond. In fact, it would be impossible to just roll over and go to sleep at that point. We cannot help but want to follow the "Amen" with a whole lot of good lovin'!

Go ahead, give it a try tonight, and see if drawing closer to God doesn't draw you incredibly closer to one another, and vice versa.

PONDER THE PRINCIPLE

◆ Have you ever wondered if there is any connection between our spirituality and our sexuality? If so, share what kind of thoughts you have considered.

◆ If you agree that there is an inseparable connection between spirituality and sexuality, do you think we draw closer to God as we draw closer to one another

CELEBRATE THE SPIRITUAL SIDE OF SEX

in marriage? Is this something that you desire to experience more fully? Why or why not?

🔥 What are some practical things you could do to draw
your spouse closer to you—both spiritually and sexually?

🔥 What are some practical things that your mate could
do to connect more intimately with you—both spiritually and sexually?

10. WILL THERE BE SEX IN HEAVEN?

All of this talk about the spiritual side of sex leads us to the question that most of us Christians have contemplated at least once in
our lives, if we are honest: Will there be sex in heaven?

Before I offer my personal opinion on the matter, based on
the research I have done, I would like to tell you about a radio
interview I did several years ago that, in all honesty, ticked me off
royally. I am not sure if the pastor who was interviewing me was
simply playing devil's advocate (if so, he wasn't a very good actor)
or if he really had this mentality, but he posed an infuriating
question. He challenged, "By telling married couples to engage
freely in sex, aren't you encouraging them to operate out of their
'sinful, animal' nature?"

Hello? I thought. *Are you serious? How could someone with theological training draw such an off-base conclusion?*

I reminded him of the order of events in Genesis and how
God created sex within marriage *before* the fall of man ever
occurred. So how in the world can it be sinful? It is only sinful in
our minds because we have let Satan steal the notion of sexuality
being a huge part of God's perfect creation. And because it *is* a

part of God's perfect creation, why in the world would we assume that there won't be sex in heaven? It is as if we assume that God is going to somehow wake up and realize, "Oh, I shouldn't have told them to do all that nasty stuff back in the garden of Eden since we won't be allowing that in heaven."

Sorry, but I cannot buy that.

Matthew 22:30 is probably another reason why we assume there won't be sex in heaven. It reads, "When people rise from the dead, they will not marry, nor will they be given to someone to marry. They will be like the angels in heaven" (NCV). In other words, there won't be any reason for marriage in heaven. Earthly marriage is intended to be a reflection of God's commitment to His bride, the Church. But once we are in heaven, there is no need for a mere reflection. We will have the Real Thing. We all will be in the presence of our heavenly Bridegroom, so our attentions and affections will no longer have to be directed toward an earthly surrogate.

But will there be *sex* in heaven? I believe the answer is both yes and no.

Let's press the pause button and consider the question, "What *is* sex?" It is not just intercourse—it is also gender. When you complete a job application and the form asks you to indicate your "sex," how do you respond? By indicating "male" or "female," of course. Will we be male and female in heaven? Why wouldn't we be? We will not be neutered at heaven's gates. Matthew 22:30 tells us that we will be as "angels," not as geldings or eunuchs. God's purpose in delivering us from a fallen world into a perfect world is to unmake the messes that *we* have made, and that Satan has made, not to unmake the perfection that *He* has made.

In addition to our sexuality remaining intact in heaven,

there is God's sexuality to consider as well. Yes, God is a sexual being, *the most sexual of all beings*, which I know sounds shocking to those of us who see sexuality as being strictly physical, but it is not. It is both physical and spiritual. Although we have historically considered God a *male* being, God actually transcends gender. He made both male *and* female "in his own image" (Genesis 1:27); therefore, God is both masculine *and* feminine in nature (a concept I explore more fully in my book *The Fantasy Fallacy: Exposing the Deeper Meaning Behind Sexual Thoughts* in a section called "Behind the Curtain: Searching for the Softer Side of God").[6] And I believe wholeheartedly that both God's *sexual* nature as well as our own sexual nature will be fully present, fully understood, and fully celebrated in heaven. It will be unadulterated, untainted, uninhibited, and we will enjoy the holiness, the purity, the perfection of all that God intended when He created us both "in His image" and sexual at the same time.

With that being established, let me provide a more direct answer by clarifying the question. What we really want to know is, *will there be physical intercourse in heaven?* Since there will be no marriage and no further need for procreation, it is doubtful. But this shouldn't be bubble-bursting news because there is so much more to the story. In the words of Dr. Peter Kreeft,

> I think there will probably be millions of more adequate ways to express love than the clumsy ecstasy of fitting two bodies together like pieces of a jigsaw puzzle. Even the most satisfying earthly intercourse between spouses cannot perfectly express *all* their love. If the possibility of intercourse in Heaven is not

actualized, it is only for the same reason earthly lovers do not eat candy during intercourse: there is something much better to do.[7]

The pleasure we experience through our God-given sexuality will perhaps be different in heaven but will most certainly be magnified exponentially. However, God will not *remove* our sexual nature. He will *redeem* it.

So rather than mourn the absence of physical sex in heaven, let us greatly anticipate the bigger sexual picture . . .

Sex on earth is like a lovely view from a cottage window. Sex in heaven will be the breathtaking view from Mount Kilimanjaro.

> The pleasure we experience through our God-given sexuality will perhaps be different in heaven but will most certainly be magnified exponentially. However, God will not *remove* our sexual nature. He will *redeem* it.

Sex on earth? A $2 box of Queen Anne chocolate-covered cherries. Sex in heaven? A bar of Amedei Porcelana (Italian chocolate, $90 per pound).

Sex on earth? A stick-figure drawing on a refrigerator door. Sex in heaven? Michelangelo's panoramas adorning the Sistine Chapel.

Sex on earth? An afternoon at the local playground. Sex in heaven? Owning Disney World.

Think of the greatest sexual pleasures imaginable—on steroids, factored exponentially to mind-boggling mathematical degrees—and we *still* are grasping at straws in comparison to the profound pleasures that await us in our heavenly home.

Dearest heavenly Father, it is enough that You save us from our sin and provide us eternal life with You, but the fact that You designed us to feel so good, both in Your presence and in the presence of our spouses, indicates that You give extraordinarily good gifts to Your children. And we are so grateful. In response to the pleasures You have created for us to fully enjoy this side of heaven and for all those pleasures You have awaiting us on the other side, we simply say . . . *Wow!*

Playing by the Rule Book

11. HOW CAN WE KNOW THAT WHAT WE ARE ■ DOING IN BED IS OKAY WITH GOD?

I WOULD LIKE TO CALL YOUR ATTENTION TO HOW THIS QUESTION is worded. It does *not* say:

- How can we know that what we are doing in bed is okay with my best friend?
- How can we know that what we are doing in bed is okay with my mother?
- How can we know that what we are doing in bed is okay with my coworkers?

Yet aren't these the ones we are sometimes tempted to ask? And in the process of asking their opinions, don't we usually share far too much about our sex life with people who have no business knowing those things about our spouses or us? The truth is that there are only three people involved in your marriage bed—you, your spouse, and God. Those are the only three people who are of any concern in the matter.

God has stated very clearly in His Word what sexual acts

are forbidden, which can be categorized as any sort of sexual involvement with someone who is not your spouse. But as far as what is appropriate inside the master bedroom (or any other room in the house) of a married couple, nothing in particular is said. Nothing about wearing sexy lingerie, or swinging from the chandelier, or talking graphically to one another, or acting out fantasies together (which we will talk more about later). Nothing.

> There are only three people involved in your marriage bed—you, your spouse, and God. Those are the only three people who are of any concern in the matter.

This is where we come to a crossroads. Are we to assume that just because God did not expressly forbid it in Scripture, it must be simply because He forgot? No. That would be heresy in my opinion. That would be humans trying to *add* to the Bible and insisting, "Thus saith the Lord . . . or at least He *should have* said it."

There was actually a group of human beings who tried that. They were called the Pharisees. They were the religious elite in Jesus' day, and they insisted on adding to the high standards to which God had already called them (specifically, through the Ten Commandments). The Pharisees tried to govern, or rather micromanage, practically everything the people did—such as when they could and could not do certain types of work, what kinds of food could be eaten or offered as a sacrifice, and what kind of cloth people could use to make their clothing. These were unnecessary burdens on people's backs, which I would bet left the Jewish people feeling like big, fat spiritual failures. Such rules kept them walking on eggshells but didn't inspire them to walk in freedom, which is why Jesus came in the first place—to set people free to worship God in spirit and in truth, not in religious hype and hypocrisy.

We can spend a lot of time stressing over possibly upsetting God in the privacy of our own bedrooms, but in light of how Scripture is silent about such things, I think the more important thing to focus on is what actually *did* make God upset.

Do you want to know what made Jesus angrier than anything else? It certainly had nothing to do with what women wore for their husbands or what sexual positions they incorporated into their lovemaking routine. It had little to do with the marriage bed at all. It was what the Pharisees were doing to God's people with their legalistic standards that were impossible to live by. They were adding to what God said was important, putting unnecessary rules and regulations on people's private and corporate lives. And all of this made Jesus furious.

And while I cannot speak for Jesus, I get pretty furious as well when I hear things from within the Christian community that sound a little something like:

- "Women shouldn't dress sexy for their husbands, or else it will awaken his appetite to look at pornography." (Funny. I can't find that in Scripture anywhere.)
- "The missionary position is the only holy way for a married couple to have sex." (Really? And what passage might that rule be found in?)
- "A man shouldn't expect his wife to have sex more often than once or twice a week, or else she'll feel 'put upon.'" (Wow! I don't recall that being preached in either the Old or New Testament, by any high priest, prophet, or apostle.)

Sentiments such as these may be well-intentioned and come from very sincere Christians who love the Lord like crazy, but one can be sincere yet still be sincerely wrong. And I believe this might be one of the reasons that most of the world does *not* look at the church as a source of real wisdom when it comes to sexual matters.

So hopefully you can understand why I am very careful not to tell people what they should or should not be doing in the bedroom. I think if I were to *add* to what God has already clearly stated, I would be guilty of Pharisaism myself. So I simply like to say, "There is *freedom* in the marriage bed!"

Say it with me—"There is *freedom* in the marriage bed!" Hallelujah!

But for those who want clear-cut, black-and-white boundary lines around that marriage bed, here is a safe-but-not-suffocating list of dos and don'ts:

Do:

- Invite God into your bedroom and ask for His blessing on your marriage bed.
- Freely engage in sex with one another as an act of worship toward our Creator.
- Ask yourself, "Was this forbidden in Scripture?" if you are inspired to do something a little different or daring. If not, then you have a yellow light. (Proceed with caution.)
- Communicate your thoughts to make sure your spouse is comfortable with your new idea. If your spouse has no objections, then you have a green light. (Go for it!)
- Always make sure your spouse feels completely safe in your presence at all times.

- Enjoy the passion and intimacy you share without guilt, shame, or inhibition.

Don't:

- Ask for or blindly receive other people's opinions about what is okay for *you* and your marriage bed. Again, this is between you, your spouse, and God.
- Make assumptions that your spouse should totally be on board with something just because *you* are comfortable with it. Everyone gets to define his or her own comfort zone.
- Belittle your partner with negative terms, such as "prude," "stick-in-the-mud," or "wet blanket," or the opposite extreme, such as "kinky" or "perverted."

We will talk more about how to resolve sexual matters that you disagree on in the next couple questions. For now, just remember that all sexual issues can be categorized in one of two ways. They are either a matter of (1) biblical mandate or (2) personal conscience. If God spoke against a particular act, then it is certainly a matter of biblical mandate, and we want to honor that for our own sake, for the sakes of our marriages, and for the sake of our relationships with God Himself. However, if it is not mentioned in Scripture, it is a matter of personal conscience. Not *someone else's* conscience but *yours*. You get to decide if it is okay with you, if it is pleasurable to you, and if it is edifying to your relationship.

So if you want to dress up to visually stimulate your spouse, no one is stopping you, especially not God. If you want to swing from the chandelier, just make sure the fixture will support you. If you want to have sex multiple times per week or even multiple times per day on occasion, knock yourselves out! In God's economy, there are no limitations placed on pleasure and passion.

◊ What specific activities have you questioned in the past as to whether they were "okay" with God or not?

◊ Do you feel as if you have greater clarity on those things after reading this section? Why or why not?

◊ Was there anything that stood out to you in the lists of "dos and don'ts" as something you really wanted to explore further with your mate? If so, what was it?

◊ Do you believe that a couple can ever be completely confident that God approves of all of their chosen sexual activities? Why or why not?

12. HOW DOES THE WHOLE *SUBMISSION* THING WORK IN MARRIAGE?

It was gut-wrenching to hear the agony and despair in my coaching client's voice as she made the reasons behind her "frigidity" crystal clear: "Why in the world should I want to have sex with a man that I can't stand the sight of?"

She wasn't frigid at all; rather, her heart had grown stone cold toward the man she had married. And as hard as it was for me to hear these words, I cannot imagine how painful they were to her husband's ears as he sat there on the couch with her. His entire body was trembling, maybe partly out of anger that she was verbally ripping him to shreds, maybe partly out of fear that their marriage was over.

Unfortunately this dynamic is not uncommon, especially in religious couples. Why? Because Christians can be experts at understanding *parts* of the Bible while completely missing other parts. In particular, most men are quite aware of the apostle Paul's words in Ephesians 5:22–24: "For wives . . . submit to your husbands as to the Lord. For a husband is the head of his wife as Christ is the head of the church. He is the Savior of his body, the church. As the church submits to Christ, so you wives should submit to your husbands in everything."

If this passage is read in isolation, it is easy to conjure up images of the stereotypical dominant male, watching a sitcom in his recliner, yelling for a sandwich, expecting sex before bed, throwing his weight around, and demanding that it's "his way or the highway." But is this what God intended? Can a man require such blind submission and servitude from a woman simply because he is the "male head of the household"? No. Respect and submission from a woman can only be *inspired*, not *required*. And the same is true with sexual interest. A husband can certainly *inspire* a woman to blossom with him in bed, but *requiring* such can be about as effective as grabbing a rosebud by its outer petals and trying to force it into full bloom. It will simply break rather than blossom if not given the time and proper nourishment to flourish.

Sometimes the relational dynamic is reversed. Husbands have also sat on my coaching couch feeling absolutely no sexual attraction to their wives at all because their wives treat them disrespectfully or even rudely. Sadly, there are many women who have some unresolved anger or resentment issues toward a previous male authority figure (such as a distant father or an abusive ex-husband or boyfriend, perhaps). This can make any sort of respectful submission difficult. If that describes you, I would say,

"Baby girl, how long are you going to drag that baggage around? You're only making life hard on yourself and your family, so how about lightening your load and seeing a counselor who can help you function more effectively in your relationships with men?" (We will talk more about sifting through an abusive past in future sections of the book.)

I have come to understand through my own life and through coaching other couples that there is a huge difference between a woman exercising the authority she shares with her husband and using her authority to bully him and others into submission. It is one thing to bless your family by taking the reins, delegating responsibilities, and effectively coleading the household. It is another to bully your family by barking out orders, demanding your own way, and demeaning anyone who does not fall into line.

As women, we are incredibly powerful creatures. And that should be a good thing. But we must learn to wield the sword of power in such a way as to protect our husbands rather than making them feel punished or overpowered. In using our power for his *benefit* rather than for his *burden*, we create a connection that bonds us together, not just emotionally but sexually as well. Wherever a woman's heart goes, her body longs to follow, and most men will confess the same thing.

Sometimes when men see that I have written books with such titles as *Every Woman's Battle* and *The Sexually Confident Wife*, they often ask, "So what did your husband do to help you become the person you are?" (Translation: *Just show me the magic wand your husband waved over you to get uninhibited sex so that I can wave it over my wife too.*)

While there is no magic wand that can be waved, there is

certainly magic in how Greg treats me and how it makes me feel. He has never yelled at me that I can recall—not even when *I* was yelling at *him*, believe it or not. I have never—not even for a moment—been fearful of his hurting me or our children. We all know Greg to be a very "soft place to land." He is one of the most laid-back people you could ever meet, and while that personality trait can drive me nuts sometimes, it is a far bigger asset than a liability. When he has concerns about something, he voices them calmly and respectfully. And he can usually win me over to his side in most arguments simply because it is hard to say no to a man's wishes when that man treats you so kindly and compassionately. He would do anything in the world for me (within reason, of course), and that inspires me to want to do anything in the world for him as well. And that eager-to-please attitude spills over into our bedroom from all other rooms in the house.

Let's take a look at a few other passages of Scripture that instruct husbands more fully on what this whole submission thing should look like in marriage. Ephesians 5:25–29 says:

> For husbands, this means love your wives, just as Christ loved the church. He gave up his life for her to make her holy and clean, washed by the cleansing of God's word. He did this to present her to himself as a glorious church without a spot or wrinkle or any other blemish. Instead, she will be holy and without fault. In the same way, husbands ought to love their wives as they love their own bodies. For a man who loves his wife actually shows love for himself. No one hates his own body but feeds and cares for it, just as Christ cares for the church.

Husbands, do you show the same tender loving care to your wife as Christ does toward us? If so, you won't need to worry that she will submit to you. A woman naturally submits to those who love, cherish, and celebrate her, especially the man who has committed his life to protecting, providing for, and serving her needs and those of her children. It is simply in our instinct to care for those who care for us.

Let's look at a couple other similar passages about the role men play in marriage:

> Husbands, love your wives and be gentle with them. (Colossians 3:19 NCV)

> In the same way, you husbands should live with your wives in an understanding way, since they are weaker than you. But show them respect, because God gives them the same blessing he gives you—the grace that gives true life. Do this so that nothing will stop your prayers. (1 Peter 3:7 NCV)

Just as my coaching client was crystal clear about her feelings, the apostle Paul makes his thoughts just as plain. Although men have been given a position of authority in their marriages and families, this leadership position leaves no room for harshness or heavy-handedness. And the 1 Peter 3:7 passage infers that the effectiveness of a man's prayers are based on how he treats his wife. I think it is safe to say that God is just as concerned with how well a man loves his wife as how well a wife submits to her husband. But my favorite verse about how the whole submission thing works in marriage is Ephesians 5:21, which says: "And further, submit to *one another* out of reverence for Christ" (italics mine).

In other words, submission is a two-way street. Just as we are both to love and serve one another, we are also to submit to one another. Imagine what that would look like in a marriage . . . how much harmony there would be in our homes . . . how much freedom from tension there would be in our families . . . how much joy we would have in our daily lives and how much spiritual growth we would experience if our energies were focused toward complementing and completing one another instead of competing to satisfy our own selfish agendas.

You could write a great love story with that kind of beautiful backdrop. In fact, you already are. You are both authors of your own marriage. I hope you will use the authority you both have been given by God to craft a marriage story worth telling and retelling for generations to come.

13. WHAT IF WE DISAGREE ON SOMETHING SEXUAL? WHO WINS THAT ARGUMENT?

Do you remember fantasizing about how great married life would be—getting all the sex you wanted, whenever you wanted it, wherever you wanted it, however you wanted it? And then you walked down the aisle and soon realized that while your fantasies may have been tension-free, your marriage bed is certainly not.

Differences of opinion about what is fun, pleasurable, interesting, safe, practical, and mutually edifying often arise in marriage. In fact, I would be shocked to learn that a couple hasn't had *any* such disagreements. (In that event, I would assume they simply have not been married long enough for tensions to surface, but give them time. They creep up eventually.)

When I have the privilege of speaking alongside my dear friend, brother, and writing partner Fred Stoeker (author of the Every Man's Battle series), I love to hear him tell the story of his first years of marriage to his beautiful wife, Brenda. He came into the relationship with certain fantasies of what married sex would be like, such as making love in the moonlight on a sand dune, taking yogurt baths together, going parking late at night. Brenda, on the other hand, didn't share *all* of Fred's fantasies, and presented some very sound reasons for refusing certain activities (such as the fact that sex in public places would be not only inappropriate and unholy, but also illegal). So Fred had a choice to make. He could either force his agenda and fulfill his desires, but run the great risk of hardening his wife's heart toward him altogether, or he could choose to respect his wife's comfort zone and honor what he calls "the essence of who Brenda is." Fortunately he made the right choice, and they not only have been happily married for thirty-two years now but also are affecting thousands of other marriages with their amazing testimonies of what God has done in their relationship.[1]

Once Fred and I were speaking together at a marriage retreat at Glen Eyrie Conference Center in Colorado Springs. As he relayed this story about submitting to his wife, the couples in attendance were moved by the power of the message and the incredible word pictures he shared. So moved, in fact, that we decided to present Fred with a token of our appreciation the next morning at breakfast.

Remember the scene at the end of the movie *A Beautiful Mind*, where all the colleagues of the Russell Crowe character gather around him at the lunch table and present him with their Montblanc pens as a sign of honor, respect, and gratitude? We staged a similar presentation at the breakfast table; only instead of expensive pens, we each presented Fred with a container of yogurt, piling them high on his plate in pyramid formation, in honor of all the yogurt baths he had sacrificed in order to show his wife that *she* was far more important than any silly fantasy he'd had. The cafeteria exploded in applause and laughter, and my heart exploded with delight to see my dear brother Fred celebrated in such a way.

But it is not always the man in the marriage who needs to lose the argument in order to win the heart of his spouse. Elizabeth's e-mail is a perfect example of what healthy sexual submission can look like in marriage:

> I had a bit of a breakthrough with my husband recently, and I know it's thanks to your book, *The Sexually Confident Wife*. Will (my husband) has asked me several times to paint my fingernails, and specifically to paint them red. I've never wanted to, and always just declined to do it without really thinking about it.
>
> I recently asked Will what intimate stuff he'd like me to be more open to, and he brought up the red fingernails thing. Immediately I felt my emotions recoiling at the idea, but for the first time, I decided to figure out the exact reason *why* I didn't want to do it rather than just decline automatically.
>
> Get this: I realized that the reason I don't like red fingernails is because the only woman I knew who typically had red fingernails was my maternal grandmother. So in my mind, red fingernails = my bitter, materialistic, and emotionally

removed grandma! What a reason to deny my husband an extremely tame fantasy of his pretty wife caressing him with her red fingernails! And I didn't even know that was the root of my aversion to them! Once I did realize it, I was able to let it go, and I painted them red the very next day and Will has been enjoying them immensely ever since! While I'm not "there" yet as far as feeling sexy about them, I certainly like what they do to my husband, so we've found common ground.

As far as what Will thinks of all this, I asked him if he's noticed any differences in me lately, and he said that he's noticed I'm a lot more forward about sex, and that he likes it because there is less "hinting around," which has often only led to disappointment and confusion.

I'm now looking more deliberately at why I do or don't do certain things sexually. I'm trying to look at the things I'm uncomfortable with from a removed, analytical perspective, and it's helping me to examine where I've gotten some of my "sexual beliefs" over the years. In doing that, I am finding that once I put aside prior bad experiences that happened to involve a certain sexual act, and put that act in the context of loving marital intimacy with my husband, some of them have actually been appealing to me for the first time in my married life!

Bravo, Elizabeth! What an example you are to all of us as we sift through sexual tensions and strive to get on the same page.

Are there things that would delight your husband or wife that you have been hesitant to try but never really understood where the hesitancy came from? If so, press the pause button on your no and take time to give some serious thought to the matter. Like Elizabeth, you might find that you have a lot more to gain by giving in than you do by standing your ground.

When you think about it, our sexuality comprises not just a handful or even a hundred different events but rather thousands of experiences throughout our lifetimes. The relationships we have been raised with, both inside and outside our homes, the movies and television shows we have watched, the music we have listened to, the billboards we have passed by, the sermons we have heard (or didn't hear), the conversations we have had with peers on school buses and in Sunday school classrooms— all of these experiences add up to a collective sexual identity.

> Our sexuality is as unique as our fingerprints.

And since no two people have lived identical lives, it only stands to reason that different experiences are going to lead to different expectations.

One of my favorite expressions is: "Our sexuality is as unique as our fingerprints." Frequently reminding ourselves of this undeniable fact can force negative thoughts (such as fear, confusion, judgment, or condemnation) toward our spouses right out of our minds. Rather than thinking of our partners as sick, twisted, or perverted because of their sexual aspirations, we can see them as adventurous, playful, or exciting. Instead of assuming that our spouses are frigid, sexual sticks-in-the-mud, or straitlaced prudes, we can respect the fact that they are self-controlled, pillars of strength, and protective of their sexual integrity.

This doesn't mean we have to bury all hopes of cultivating the rich, rewarding sex lives we long for when our spouses are a little more on the conservative end of the spectrum than we might prefer. We can still work toward building greater levels of trust and confidence in our marriage partners such that they may change their minds in the future. Nor does it mean that we have to become sexual doormats if our spouses lean more toward the liberal end of the sexual spectrum, giving in to anything and everything they conjure up. We can still have healthy boundaries and only agree to what makes us comfortable.

By viewing your partner's sexuality through a nonjudgmental lens, you are able to make him or her feel respected, safe, celebrated, cherished, and loved. Isn't that one of the main goals of marriage?

Dearest Lord, may I never insist on having my own way at the expense of my partner's comfort zone. Show me how to help my spouse feel so safe in our marriage bed that blossoming comes naturally. Give us both patience and passion as we express our love for each other, and may You be glorified and honored by all the pleasure we experience in our intimate times together. Thank You for the many gifts we have in our marriage and in our marriage bed. Amen.

PASSION PRINCIPLE #2:

Celebrate the Mental Side of Sex

Sex on the Brain

14. WHY DO HUMANS THINK ABOUT SEX SO MUCH?

In the summer of 1999, we took our young children for an afternoon outing to the Caldwell Zoo in Tyler, Texas. As we entered an area called the Texas Petting Zoo, Erin and Matthew were thrilled over the thought that they actually would be getting hands-on experience with the animals. Our first stop was the Longhorn cattle pen, where several dozen parents and children waited their turn to pet the new baby calf, which just happened to be tucked up underneath his mama's udders for an afternoon snack. My three-year-old son watched this scene in amazement, then boldly inquired of me in his loudest outdoor voice, "Mama, did *you* do that to *me* when you was a cow?"

Every adult within earshot giggled, and I had to join them. It was an honest question, so I gave an honest answer and replied, "Matthew, I actually *did* feel like a cow when I was doing that to you!" The giggling turned to guffaws of laughter, and thus a precious memory was made that afternoon.

Matthew learned not only how baby calves and baby boys are fed by their mothers but also how baby animals are made. It seemed as though every cage we encountered was filled with animals in heat. The giraffes were necking; the gazelles were horny; the camels were humping. It was as if someone spiked the hay with some powerful aphrodisiac. And there was, of course, an inquiring child in the crowd always wanting to know, "What are those two animals *doing*?"

Although humans are certainly on a much higher intellectual and spiritual plane than animals, our basic physical instincts are really not very different. We have four main activities we naturally gravitate toward over and over—eating, drinking, sleeping, and sexually connecting with our mates. It is simply how God wired us, and it is a beautiful thing if you consider the big-picture purposes He had in mind.

Why did God wire us for hunger and thirst? So we wouldn't starve to death or get dehydrated and make ourselves sick. So our bodies could thrive and manufacture the energy we need to function when we respond to these natural instincts with healthy food and water.

Why did God wire us for sleep? So our bodies and brains could rest and get reenergized for another day of living for His glory. So we could go about our days feeling refreshed, at least until our batteries needed to be recharged once again.

Why did God wire us for sex? Here are just a few reasons:

- to bring beautiful babies into the world
- so our bodies and brains could experience intense physical pleasure
- to release stress and tension
- to medicate emotional pain
- so our hearts and spirits would feel intimately connected and passionately bonded to another human being

- so we would feel passionately loved, and have a powerful way of communicating to another that he or she is deeply loved as well

Most of us can accept our hunger, our thirst, and our need for sleep as perfectly natural, but the fact that we are sexual creatures can be hard to accept, at least not without a certain degree of guilt. But do we ever feel guilty for experiencing true hunger several times a day? Or genuine thirst? Do we ever feel sinful for growing sleepy every eighteen hours or so? Of course not. It is how our bodies function, and like those zoo animals, we don't waste much time analyzing it at all. We just feed those needs in order to satisfy ourselves.

So why do we waste time and energy analyzing, justifying, fretting, or feeling guilty over our sexual needs and desires? Seems silly, doesn't it? (Or perhaps you are like me and find human sexuality so fascinating that you can't help but waste a lot of time and energy analyzing it.)

I believe the reason we worry about our sexuality is because we have somehow bought the lie that sex is dirty, shameful, base, animalistic, and hedonistic rather than natural, instinctual, spiritual, sublime, and holy. As a result, some of us have lost our ability to accept, embrace, or celebrate that facet of our humanity. Instead, we may shudder with shock and embarrassment to seriously consider how often our brains entertain sexual thoughts. In fact, many of us wish we could just flip a switch and never think of sex at all. Some have actually mastered a variety of techniques that allow them to do just that—to ignore and neglect their natural, God-given sexuality altogether. While I am certainly not trying to shame anyone, I think the fact that we have grown so adept at absolutely starving our natural sexual desires is, indeed, a crying shame.

But what if we learned to accept the fact that God has created us as sexual beings, and a natural, healthy sex drive comes part and parcel with that blueprint? That sexual thoughts are as natural as a hunger pang? Or a dry mouth? Or sleepy eyes? What if we could grow as comfortable with and ecstatic over a delightful afternoon tryst in our marriage bed as we are with, say, a plateful of our favorite holiday foods, a cup of hot cocoa or apple cider, and an afternoon nap to ease the calorie-induced coma? Yes, it is possible to enjoy sex as freely as we indulge in satisfying these other natural cravings.

> We have somehow bought the lie that sex is dirty, shameful, base, animalistic, and hedonistic rather than natural, instinctual, spiritual, sublime, and holy.

We must grasp the fact that God placed these human desires in us for a reason—for *many* divine reasons. If we had no internal compass pointing us toward food, couldn't we starve to death? If we had no recurring thoughts of drinking liquids, we would dehydrate within forty-eight hours. No natural gravitational pull toward a pillow would mean becoming physically exhausted to the point of delirium within a few short days. Although individuals can live without sex for long periods of time, or even a lifetime if they so choose, let's think in terms of the bigger picture. What if humans in general did not have any sort of sexual appetite at all? What would happen? Not only would we become painfully disconnected and isolated from one another, but the human race would eventually die off within a century or so. Heaven forbid!

God gave us natural, healthy appetites for everything that

our minds, bodies, and souls *need*. These appetites guarantee our optimum survival. As such, these appetites are certainly a blessing, not a burden. So let's embrace, cherish, and celebrate them fully.

PONDER THE PRINCIPLE

- How do you feel about the fact that you have a natural recurring appetite for sexual arousal, stimulation, and fulfillment?
- Have you ever wanted to just turn your sexuality switch to the *off* position? Do you think it is even possible to do that? Why or why not?
- If your sexual appetite has been ignored or starved for a while, are you willing to feed it once again so that it (and your marriage relationship) can thrive?

15. WHY DO I SO RARELY/OFTEN THINK ABOUT SEX IN COMPARISON TO MY SPOUSE?

As mentioned in the previous question, it is only natural for humans to think about sex. However, when one spouse thinks about sex far more than the other, the resulting libido differences can become a major issue. We will discuss more about how to balance mismatched sex drives in question 35, but for now let's discuss why we can be so different in this department.

I have been on both sides of this fence, as have many married folks. There have been times when I would hit a wall sexually and have little to no interest and other seasons when I felt more like climbing a wall, due to my abundance of interest.

There have also been many occasions when Greg was having recurrent cravings for a sexual connection and others when his brain was driven to distraction to the point that sex simply was not on his radar.

We have found that the key to surviving these fluctuating seasons and pendulum swings from one extreme to the other is . . . drumroll, please . . . *not* to take it personally! If you are the one feeling the sting of rejection, it is most likely not about *you* at all. And if you are the one experiencing a temporary lull in your libido, it is not a sign that your relationship is sinking like the *Titanic*. Most likely, these differences in sexual thought patterns have more to do with hormone production than anything else, and hormone production is not always something that we are able to control.

Before I launch into an explanation about male and female hormones, let me go on the record as saying that I try to avoid sexual stereotypes at all costs. Gross overgeneralizations such as, "Men think about sex all the time, and women never do" can be not only very wrong, but very hurtful, especially for the wife who wonders, "Why isn't *my* husband one of those men who thinks about sex just as often (if not more so) than me?" If that is you, sweet sister, please sit tight with me until we get to some of the future questions about practical ways to float each other's boats and light each other's fires, okay? But for now, let's get back to male and female hormones.

In her incredibly insightful book called *The Female Brain*, Dr. Louann Brizendine explains why certain sexual stereotypes may exist in the first place. She makes several observations about a woman's brain in comparison to a man's brain that might account for some of the discrepancies in how often we each think sexual thoughts. For example:

- The sex-related centers of the male brain are twice as large as those of the female brain, which explains why men think about sex many times throughout the day, whereas women may only think about it once or twice a day.[1]
- Testosterone is the hormone responsible for fueling our sexual thoughts, and the male body naturally produces ten to one hundred times more testosterone than the female body.[2]
- When stress levels are high (as they often are in life, marriage, parenting, career), men respond by thinking of sex more often. Women, however, respond to stress by producing a hormone called cortisol, which abruptly shuts off their desire for sex and physical touch.[3]

So, biologically speaking, men are naturally wired to think of sex far more often than women. Also, as our marital relationships progress and we start families, our sexual thought patterns naturally evolve as well. For instance:

- The euphoria of romantic love and intensity of sexual interest usually lasts somewhere between six months and approximately two years. Beyond that, the brain produces less dopamine and oxytocin (the hormones responsible for drawing the two of you together sexually like magnets). Therefore, the mental need to remain locked in each other's embrace lessens substantially.[4]
- From within two weeks of conceiving a child, a woman's brain chemistry is radically altered, shifting its focus from her sexual partner to her developing baby, and after birth

takes place, breast-feeding can easily replace or interfere with a new mother's desire for her partner.[5]

In other words, the honeymoon isn't intended to last forever. The *new* wears off eventually, and our long-term reality usually proves different from our short-term fantasies of what marriage would be like. Then throw children into the mix, and it is easy to observe how a woman's obsession with her children can put an even bigger damper on her sexual thoughts toward her husband for many years (or decades) to come. Similarly, a man's obsession with his career can have the same effect. Both husbands and wives must intentionally make room for, and keep mental space available for, fueling the one relationship that is most important to our long-term well-being. Think about it. Kids grow up and leave the nest. Careers evolve and eventually come to an end. Friendships often fade. But our marriage—that is a *forever* thing, so we may need to adjust our expectations after that euphoric honeymoon phase disappears in our rear-view mirror.

The encouraging reality, however, is that even when our brains no longer produce that sexual high that we initially enjoy so much, it does not mean that love has to grow cold. It simply means our bodies are not designed to maintain revved-up states of passionate love. Our relationships must evolve into more stable, mature states that can be maintained for long periods of time.

When viewed in this light, even this relational evolution can be cause for celebration. Although your heads may not be spinning any longer or nearly as often, neither of you are going to throw in the towel just because mental interest in your sex life levels out. That's for relational lightweights whose marriages are like rain puddles—sparkly on the surface but not very deep. Two mature people who are fully committed to each other for life will learn *both* the art of making love and the art of making love last.

One of the ways Greg and I have tried to make love last is by realizing that "being horny" is not the only reason to have sex. After all, there are many seasons of life when we just do not have a lot of time or energy for being turned on. So, instead, we experienced a major sexual paradigm shift. With every little reason to celebrate (good news, job promotions, family accomplishments, answers to prayer), having sex with each other simply makes the occasion feel all the more special. When we come home from work stressed, sex can de-stress us to a great degree. If we are feeling lethargic, a few minutes of sex followed by a little basking in the afterglow can recharge our batteries and help us make it through the rest of the evening. When one of us is feeling blue, sexual intimacy brings great comfort to us both. So thinking of having sex is not something we do just when we physically crave sexual release. Thinking of sex has become a way of bonding ourselves together in a very intimate, powerful way—through both the good times and the bad.

Father God, give us Your vision for healthy sexuality. Show us the power it holds to bond us together spiritually, mentally, emotionally, and physically. Give us a supernatural sensitivity, teaching us to truly minister to each other's deepest needs through a more intimate connection. In Jesus' name we pray, amen.

16. WHAT IS THE DIFFERENCE BETWEEN LOVE AND LUST?

Ever since my husband was three years old, he has had recurring nightmares of a man entering his room while he is sleeping. This man has a big, sharp sword in his hand, and he is always intent on stabbing Greg with it. Needless to say, Greg was very afraid of the man with the sword and tried to stay as far away from him as possible in order to protect himself.

It wasn't until years later when Greg matured that he understood that the man was a doctor, the sword was a hypodermic syringe, and the man's intention was to inject Greg with necessary medications in treating an extreme case of meningitis Greg had actually contracted as a toddler. The man wasn't trying to hurt or kill Greg but help him heal and give him a chance at a full life. What Greg thought was a great evil was actually one of his greatest allies.

> Our greatest ally, our sexuality, is too often seen as our greatest evil.

I think we have done a similar thing with sexual desire. Our greatest ally, our sexuality, is too often seen as our greatest evil. For decades we have been taught that sexual desire is predatory, dirty, raunchy, nasty, inappropriate, scary, and abusive—just to name a few adjectives. Those of us who were raised to believe these things have tried to keep our sexuality at bay as best we can because we perceived that *all* sexual thoughts, feelings, and actions must be taboo and sinful.

Boy, were we off base! Do we really think that God was just trying to trip us up and make us fall into sin when He created us as sexual beings? Absolutely not! But perhaps these misconceptions explain why I often receive e-mails, from both men and women, sharing something along the lines of . . .

- "I don't want to stare at my wife too much, or else I'll just start burning with lust."
- "Is it bad that I look at my husband's body and think all kinds of kinky sexual thoughts?"
- "I truly believed getting married would cure me of my lust, but I still want sex with my wife practically all the time."

In case you didn't notice, each of these people has sadly mistaken love as lust. They have thought that something perfectly natural was completely perverted and believed that they were wretchedly sinful creatures for simply experiencing the holy urges that God wove into the fibers of our being. But there is nothing lustful about what any of them have presented.

It is important that we understand the difference between *love* and *lust* so we will know when we are crossing the line and when we are perfectly within appropriate boundaries. There is no need to be fearful of something that ultimately brings us health and life—and nothing brings health and life into a marriage like sexual chemistry.

Let's make it fun and put it in the form of a quiz. Answer "Love" if you think this is a healthy relational dynamic, but answer "Lust" if you think it is a violation of our sexual and spiritual integrity:

1. For a married man to look at his wife, notice what a gorgeous woman she is, and long to be with her sexually as a result—*Love* or *Lust*?

2. For a married woman to drink her husband in through her eyes and ears and allow erotic thoughts to flow through her mind as a result—*Love* or *Lust*?

3. For a couple to satisfy their sexual appetites through an intimate encounter, yet still long for more and more connection with one another—*Love* or *Lust*?

The answers? *Love*—on all three counts. Why in the world would anyone think any of these things are forbidden? Just because a thought, feeling, or action is sexual does not mean it is sinful. We must be able to distinguish between the two if we are going to be good stewards of our sexuality.

One of the best definitions of *lust* I have ever heard came from James Robison during a television interview I was doing with him and his lovely wife, Betty, on *Life Today*. James said, "Lust isn't noticing that something is sexually attractive. We can't help but do that because God is the Creator of such stunning beauty! Lust is being manipulative and trying to make something yours that simply doesn't belong to you."

Your spouse, however, *does* belong to you, so letting him or her turn your head and turn you on over and over is perfectly okay. In fact, it is cause for celebration. It's when we try to lure someone who does not belong to us into some sort of sexual or emotional entanglement that we are on shaky ground. For example, how would you answer these scenarios?

- Going out of your way to pass by the desk of a married coworker because you find him or her so attractive and fun to banter with—*Love* or *Lust*?

- Attending a local restaurant where the waitresses dress a little on the provocative side because you enjoy the scenery—*Love* or *Lust?*
- Alleviating boredom by searching online for an old flame to reconnect with, just for some laughs and a stroll down memory lane (and maybe an ego boost or two)—*Love* or *Lust?*

Yeah, it doesn't take a brain surgeon to dissect those questions and figure out that lust is at the root of each one of them. When we explore ways to get our egos stroked by someone we are not married to, trouble brews. But when we focus all our sexual energies on cultivating a rich, rewarding relationship with the one person with whom we are allowed to have a rip-roaring good time, as often as we want, there is absolutely nothing lustful about that. So stop fretting with false guilt, start staring at the beautiful person you are married to, and feel the freedom to enjoy one another completely.

Getting on the Same Page

17. HOW DID WE GET SUCH DIFFERENT IDEAS ABOUT SEX AND LOVE?

"I JUST WANT TO FEEL CONNECTED TO MY HUSBAND!" GINA CRIED in my coaching office.

The next day I met with both Gina and her husband. Upon digging a little deeper, I learned that Connor felt the same way. He wanted to connect more often with his wife, too, and was quite frustrated that he kept trying and trying to do just that, only to be rejected by her. So how is it possible for a couple to want the exact same thing, yet both of them feel so unsuccessful in that endeavor?

First I asked Gina to define the word *connection*.

"I want to feel close to him. I want us to talk more. I want us to pray together more. I want to feel as if we're best friends," she replied.

Then I asked her what she thought Connor's definition of *connection* might be. After a long pause it was as if a lightbulb went off in her brain, and she boldly declared, "Sex!"

Connor shook his head up and down frantically like a baby kangaroo with ADHD on a sugar high after a birthday party.

He was saying, "I'd feel more emotionally connected to you if you were more willing to connect physically with me."

She was saying, "I'd feel more physically connected to you if you were more emotionally connected with me."

Another couple, Kim and Rick, say it took several years after having kids to work through their different ideas of sex and love. Kim explained, "I felt tired and worn-out after spending the day taking care of little kids and nursing a baby. The *last* thing I wanted was sex." As a result, Rick grew distant because he felt as though his wife didn't want him. Neither of them knew how to verbalize their feelings to each other without sounding selfish, but after a few months of being intimate only every couple of weeks, Rick spoke up.

"I just don't feel connected to you, Kim. I know you are tired, but I need you to save enough energy for me. Sex is what makes me feel connected to you."

Kim says she was very frustrated at his comment because it seemed to require that she add to her ever-growing to-do list.

"It wasn't that I didn't want to feel connected to my husband. I just had nothing left to give physically. But he just couldn't understand how having sex felt like something I *had* to do, not really something I longed to do."

It is bewildering how a husband and wife can have the exact same goal but a different strategy entirely. So how *did* husbands and wives get such different ideas about sex and love?

Let's consider the unique roles God gave men and women. God designed men as the progenitors of the human race. They are wired to ensure the continuation of the generations. How? Through their healthy sex drive. As long as men want sex, babies will be made. And this is a good thing. Hooray for the male sex drive! Hooray for the beautiful babies that result! Hooray for the families formed!

Women, on the other hand, are designed by God as the nurturers of the human race. They are wired to ensure that babies grow up to be healthy creatures. How? By caring for their every need. Think mama cat constantly cleaning her kittens. Think mama bear protecting her cubs from any threat of harm. Think mama bird getting up early for the worm so she can feed the babies in the nest. Moms serve as great go-to gals for just about anything their kids need, and this is a good thing as well. Hooray for hands-on, emotionally available moms!

So because men are driven to fulfill their roles through their sex drive, they naturally crave physical connection. And because women are driven to fulfill their roles through their emotional drive, they naturally long to feel relationally and emotionally close to others.

To be fair, sometimes it is the husband who craves more emotional connection or a wife who clamors for more sexual intimacy. Either way, when the two compete against each other—holding out until their own needs or desires are met— no one wins. Both the husband and wife lose, and their children often lose too. But if they can learn to celebrate their own unique wiring and the unique wiring of their spouse, they can experience great joy in both the giving and receiving of the fulfillment they crave.

PONDER THE PRINCIPLE

◆ What is your idea of "connection" in marriage?
◆ On a scale of 1 to 10 (1 being far apart, and 10 being

closely connected) how would you rate your connection during this current season of life?

🔥 Describe a season of marriage when you felt most connected.

🔥 Specifically, what do you need from your spouse to feel more closely connected to him or her?

18. HOW CAN WE GET IN THE MOOD FOR SEX MORE OFTEN?

This question is both incredibly complex and incredibly simple to answer at the same time. It is complex in that it has several layers, but those layers can basically be categorized into four simple questions:

- What turns a wife on sexually?
- What turns a wife off sexually?
- What turns a husband on sexually?
- What turns a husband off sexually?

It can be incredibly easy to find the answers to all four of these questions. How? By simply *asking* each other to answer them personally.

As much as I wish I could unravel the mystery of why an individual or a couple doesn't seem to have sex more often, that would be about as impossible as *you* describing the sexual dynamic in *my* marriage relationship to me. No one can decipher that code except the couple involved.

So it is going to be up to you to answer this question for yourselves. To get the conversation started, I polled several husbands and wives and asked them to tell me both what turned them on to one another and what turned them off. See if you agree with any of their answers.

The men's responses could be summed up in these three statements:

- "I don't expect my wife to look like a supermodel by any stretch of the imagination, and I know that having four children will certainly take its toll on a woman's body, but I appreciate how my wife really tries to look and feel her best by eating relatively healthy and staying active. *That's* sexy to me."
- "My biggest libido killer is when my wife won't stop nagging or criticizing. I know I'm not perfect, and she has a right to be upset with me at times, but when she never lets up long enough to connect with me sexually, I feel like a total failure, and I certainly don't feel inspired to be intimate with her on any level."
- "I don't want to have to be the one to initiate sex every time. She should pursue me as well. I need to know that she wants to be intimate with me, not just as a response to my own sexual frustrations, but in response to her own desire for me."

As you can see, the men's answers were relatively simple—for a woman to take care of herself physically, to take care of him emotionally, and to take some initiative sexually.

Women, however, were far more detailed in their descriptions of what floated their sexual boats and what didn't. She gets turned off, too tired, or too distracted when . . .

1. she is exhausted from the day's activities and the evening routine
2. she feels she didn't have the support she needed in getting kids to bed on time
3. she is thinking about her to-do list for the next day
4. either partner has bad breath
5. the bedroom is untidy or uninspiring
6. there is too much slobber (or other bodily fluids) involved
7. she is worried that children will walk in
8. he accidentally hits, kicks, pinches, or knees her in tender places
9. he hasn't talked with her much or prayed with her lately
10. she feels cold and just wants to go to sleep under the warm covers

Yeah, call us "high maintenance," but a woman likes to have her physical, mental, emotional, and spiritual needs met before she can get her sexual pilot light burning. So here are some practical tips for couples in case any of the items on this list are an issue for you:

1. Men, remember that sex starts in the kitchen. Offer to help with dishes, children's baths, or whatever else your wife may need to juggle before jumping into bed that night, and hopefully she will be inspired to "reward her hero" rather than feeling that she got zero help from you.
2. Make a rule with your kids that "homework help" expires at 9 p.m. (or whatever time is appropriate for your child's age) so that your late-night hours are not spent engrossed in math problems or science projects.

3. Wives, before heading to bed, jot down things you need to be sure to remember the next day. Then you won't be tempted to keep those distracting thoughts in your head once it hits the pillow.

4. Buy a bottle of Scope or Listerine to keep handy in the bathroom for nightly use before crawling into bed.

5. Get the dirty laundry off the floor, the clean laundry off the bed, and so forth, so that things feel "settled" in the bedroom. Lighting a candle, or two or ten, is a super-simple way to create some mojo magic. Also pay attention to scents, using lavender, vanilla, or musk air fresheners, which are ranked as the most sexually appealing. And if a master bedroom makeover is called for, what a great investment—a few days, a couple hundred dollars, and you have a room that draws you inside more often.

6. Keep a stack of clean washcloths in your nightstand drawer for quick cleanups when juices start flowing a little too freely.

7. Install a lock on the door, and rest easy that you won't be having any surprise visitors in the heat of the moment.

8. Leave a bedside lamp on so your husband can *see* where he is putting his hands and knees; then unexpected injury isn't as likely.

9. Husbands, never start the conversation with, "Do you want to have sex?" Begin with "How was your day?" or "Have I told you lately how wonderful you are?" or "Do you have any idea how much I love you?" You get the idea. Warm her up before expecting her to sizzle with you.

And speaking of sizzling, that last thing on the list of turn-offs ("she feels cold") is one for which I created a special blog post. I recently learned that women simply cannot orgasm when they are cold. No, it is not just in your head, ladies—it is a biological fact. Orgasm requires mental focus and concentration as well as physical relaxation, both of which are next to impossible when we are shivering. So here are a few practical tips to keep you warm so you can keep things hot between you and hubby:

1. Put a space heater in your room about an hour before bedtime to bring the temperature up to comfortable levels. Also, turn off the ceiling fan as you are climbing into bed.
2. Do some light exercises at the end of the day—a few jumping jacks or sit-ups—just enough to get your blood circulation going in order to warm your body naturally.
3. Take a hot shower or bath right before bed so the cooler air is a welcome relief.
4. Get creative with what kind of pajamas you wear to bed, such as button-up (or un-buttoned-up) pajama tops that make certain body parts easily accessible to him while keeping other parts (shoulders, back, arms) warm.
5. Get creative with your covers, such as making a tent, using your knees as tent poles but draping the blanket down in the middle so certain parts of your anatomy are within reach. (If we can do it for the ob-gyn, we can do it for our husbands.)
6. It may not be his idea of the sexiest look, but keep your fuzzy socks on if necessary. Feet are the body parts that are most prone to cold because of the distance blood is required to travel to keep them warm.

7. Heat a bottle of lotion in the microwave and ask your husband for a hot foot massage or back rub. I can't imagine he wouldn't be obliged if he knew where you were headed with the idea.

Now let's recap: a little cooperation and communication, a scratch pad and pen, a bottle of mouthwash, a few candles, a stack of washcloths, a door lock, a pair of fuzzy socks, a bottle of lotion . . . add your own helpful items to this list. Total cost for most of these items? Far less than the cost of marriage counseling when your sex life is not what you both want it to be. So spend a few moments contemplating what turns you on sexually versus what turns you off, open those lines of communication, and create the sexual and emotional connection you both desire.

19. IS IT REALLY POSSIBLE TO BE "NAKED AND FEEL NO SHAME"?

Although there are many hurdles that often hold couples back in the bedroom, there is one in particular that outweighs (no pun intended) them all. Yep—body image issues.

Before I dive into this topic, let me clarify that when the Bible says Adam and Eve were both naked and felt no shame (Genesis 2:25), this refers to far more than just being comfortable in their birthday suits. But for the sake of brevity, I would like to zero in on what a negative body image can do to the freedom and lack of inhibition we should be able experience in the bedroom. And when it comes to body image issues, I am not talking about just women—men have them too. They often feel as if their frames are too small, their guts are too large, or they simply lack the definition of the super-cut guy with six-pack abs on the P90X commercials. He can get really self-conscious when he develops "Dunlap's Disease" because his belly has "dun lapped" over his belt. I had to laugh when I recently heard a pastor in New Zealand declare, "My wife tells me I have the body of a god. His name is Buddha!" I was glad he could laugh about it, too, but I do wonder if a man's sexual self-esteem isn't negatively affected by such physical characteristics that are not considered ideal by our looks-obsessed culture.

As of this writing my fifty-year-old husband is fretting over the fact that his chest hair is turning gray and his hairline is rapidly receding. Regardless of my reminders that I like an older, distinguished-looking man and that he will always be sexy to me no matter how much hair he loses or wrinkles he gains, it is still difficult for him to accept the fact that age is taking its toll on his body, just as it does on everyone. I will say, however, that although men can certainly be plagued by a negative body image, many seem to be able to compartmentalize that issue long enough to let down their hair (receding hairlines, bald spots, and all) in the bedroom and have great fun.

Ladies, I'm just wondering—why couldn't we learn to do the same thing? Think about it. We rarely find our male counterparts cowering in the corner of the bedroom, clinging to a fuzzy robe, and crying, "You can't possibly think I'm sexy!" Men can usually compartmentalize how they feel about their physical appearance long enough to wholeheartedly declare, "Hey, baby! Bring it ON!" in the bedroom.

Unfortunately I can't say the same thing about most women. It is amazing how we let such tiny things have such a big impact on our marriage bed, things such as . . .

· being too tall	· being too short	· being too fat	· being too thin
· small breasts	· big breasts	· saggy breasts	· lactating breasts
· pudgy tummies	· cellulite ripples	· stretch marks	· C-section scars
· bubble butts	· flat butts	· wide hips	· no hips
· full thighs	· bird legs	· cankles	· spider veins
· thin hair	· thick hair	· straight hair	· curly hair
· pale skin	· dark skin	· freckles	· moles
· crow's feet	· laugh lines	· acne scars	· age spots

And my guess is that any woman reading this book can most likely add her own unique insecurities to this list.

But here is the question: Can a woman learn to freely share her body with her husband without fear or shame creeping in and killing the mood? Can she set her own insecurities aside long enough to go full throttle, losing herself in her husband's loving embrace and sharing herself completely? I believe no matter where a woman feels she falls on the spectrum of too *this* or too *that*, she can learn to love the skin she is in—and the effect that skin can have on her husband and marriage when she confidently shares it with him.

For example, although Charissa struggled with an eating disorder most of her life and once had an incredibly hard time even looking at herself in the mirror without hating the reflection, marriage has proven to be a magical elixir to cure many of her inhibitions. On her blog (www.charissasteyn.com) she writes:

> I remember that first day my husband ever saw me in a bikini. Every layer seemed painful to take off. I refrained from making eye contact with him, for fear he'd see the shame in my eyes.
>
> Nevertheless, he took in all of me. More than a quick glance, it felt like an intrusive stare, the kind that peered straight into

my soul. Although I wanted to run away, I could feel that God was healing my heart.

I have learned that letting my husband gaze at me is one of the keys to a healthy body image and sexual self-esteem. No longer is he looking at me with my bikini. Now he is perusing every inch of my bare body. And he wants to do it all the time, even when I'm having a not-so-beautiful day. Contrary to making comments on my bloated belly or the bumps on my bum, he only gazes . . . longingly . . . just as he did that day by the pool.

Even in lovemaking we have discovered the power of keeping our eyes open, lights on, and sheets off! Although it was nerve-racking at first, letting my husband peruse every nook and cranny of my body has become a source of freedom for me. Silencing the shame in my head, his eyes drip with pure acceptance and adoration. He is full of curiosity, bursting with love, and excited to explore every part of me.

Husbands, recognize that it was how Charissa's husband responded to her vulnerability and willingness to share her (naked) body that gave her the freedom to do it often. Unfortunately I hear from other wives how their husbands are often critical, even cruel, as they compare their wives to some supermodel and complain about how they don't measure up—as if that is going to inspire them to open up and share the bodies God has given them.

Gentlemen, do yourselves a favor and get a clue if you haven't already. Not even supermodels really look like those photos you may want to compare your wife to. Digital media and airbrushing create an impossible standard for any woman to live up to, and the comparisons themselves are a major libido killer. If you want flawless, ageless perfection, marry a bronze statue. But if you want a real woman who can love you back and grow old gracefully with you, embrace and celebrate every part of her through every season of life, and hopefully she will develop the freedom to do the same.

Ladies, I also want to urge you not to wait until your husband makes you feel beautiful and sexy before you begin seeing yourself that way. How *you* feel about yourself is the biggest factor in how much freedom you will feel in your marriage bed. It is not up to someone else to make you feel good about your own body. That is a gift only you can give yourself.

> It is not up to someone else to make you feel good about your own body. That is a gift only you can give yourself.

Terrica has been on a marvelous journey to give herself such a gift. I will let her explain why and how:

I'm irrevocably convinced there isn't a woman on the planet who hasn't struggled with body image at some point in life. I make that statement with sincere conviction. Several years ago, as a married twenty-something, I signed on as Shannon's research assistant for her book, *The Sexually Confident Wife*. For months I researched everything from magazine articles to scientific studies and even celebrity testimonies, and regardless of the source, if the topic was female body image, the conversation was negative. I was blown away.

Growing up with my own weight and confidence struggles, I understood the issue well, but what I didn't realize was how overwhelmingly prevalent it is in even the most unexpected places (like Hollywood). As my research continued, so did confession after vulnerable confession of women I considered breathtakingly beautiful, from my closest friends and family to flawless faces that graced magazine covers from week to week. To be honest, it made me downright furious! They were all buying into such lies and propaganda. And I found myself in no way innocent.

On the contrary, I saw myself so clearly among them, heard my own voice distinctly among theirs chanting the same complaints, professing the same lies over myself day in and day out. It was devastating and embarrassing.

Somewhere in the midst of those many months of research, finally sick of the emotional roller coaster that body image issues provoked in me, I made a decision: the ride was over. I wouldn't be subject to it anymore, simple as that. As a vibrant, healthy young woman, I realized this mentality was literal insanity, and I was determined to change it.

I made the decision to get more comfortable than ever in my skin. I'd close the blinds and walk around my apartment naked on occasion, just because. I began speaking life over myself, quoting Scripture, expressing gratitude to God for precisely how He made me. If I caught myself thinking negative thoughts, I would immediately stop and replace them with positive ones. I took myself for long introspective walks and intentional shopping trips to pick up gourmet ingredients to create delicious and healthy meals, understanding that nourishing myself, both soul and body, was imperative. I wanted to feel good primarily, trusting the rest to follow. I combed through books and blogs and articles, educating myself on anything and everything health related.

Essentially, I unashamedly divorced my cultural view of health and beauty and re-created it from the inside out, but this time with knowledge, understanding, and fear of the

Lord. I passionately desired to honor Him in how I treated this body and this life, both His very intimate creations.

By the way, at the time of this writing, I sit at my keyboard eight and a half months pregnant with my first child, and I can honestly say that I have never felt more beautiful. The hips and thighs I lamented through adolescence are today serving a beautiful purpose I never could have fathomed, preparing to literally bring my child into the world. The breasts I feared were too small at one point and too large at another now cause me to marvel, as soon they'll serve to nourish a tiny new life. The stomach I cursed for doing nothing more than being has miraculously expanded each day to accommodate the growth of a tiny girl I'll soon love more than life.

Today, I could not be more grateful for every single curve of this intricately, lovingly designed vessel, and I cannot wait to blissfully pass along such knowledge and truth to the very daughter this body now wondrously carries.

Yes, I cried when I read those words on her blog (http://terricajoy .com). I get so delighted to hear of women falling in love—not just with a man but with themselves. There is absolutely no reason *not* to when you think of the awesome body God has given you and the amazing way it functions to bring life to yourself and those you love.

Oh, if every woman could respect her body in such a way, honor her God in such a way, and bless her husband in such a way. Remember, God didn't just make our breasts and hips and vaginas to make babies. He created them for our *pleasure*. For our husbands' pleasure. And yes, even for God's pleasure as we learn to love both the Creator and His marvelous creation.

Lord Jesus, help us stop comparing ourselves to others and feeling as if we can never measure up. Show us how to respect and appreciate the beautiful bodies You have given us. Inspire an attitude of gratitude for the wonderful ways our strong bodies function to accomplish many things each day. And remind us of the awesome power we possess to strengthen our marriages when we freely share our bodies with our spouses. In Your precious name we pray, amen.

Rules of (Mental) Engagement

20. IS IT POSSIBLE TO STOP THINKING SEXUAL THOUGHTS?

BEFORE DIVING INTO THIS QUESTION, I WANT TO TELL YOU ABOUT a shocking phone call I received. The voice on the other end of the line was quite feeble, and I could tell the person was on up in years. She said she had just read some of my books and wanted to know if I would be interested in hearing her testimony. Intrigued, I urged her to please go ahead.

She had been married more than fifty years, but she and her husband almost didn't make it past the thirty-year point. They were headed to divorce court when her husband begged, "Would you *please* be willing to see a counselor about your sexual hang-ups?"

Although willing to share in the responsibility of their crumbling marriage, he felt as if so many of their problems stemmed from a stunted sexual connection. As she shared her fears and insecurities with her counselor about "letting go" in bed, she insisted, "I know God would be so displeased with all of those sexual thoughts running through my head, and I *don't* want to displease God!"

The counselor inquired as to what types of thoughts plagued her in those moments and found them to be rather normal, run-of-the-mill mental patterns. No one had ever explained to this woman that, because orgasm is 95 percent mental for women, our brains naturally entertain arousing thoughts while being physically aroused by our husbands. He wisely asked, "If God designed your body and your brain in such a way that they work together in unison to provide sexual pleasure to both you and your husband, isn't that a *good* thing? Isn't that the way God intended for the human body to work? Why would you expect to operate any differently?"

He also posed the question, "Do you think that God would be any *less* displeased with your decision to divorce due to sexual inhibitions?"

> We can feel grateful rather than guilty, as long as we are using the sexual energy created within to fuel the home fires, not start a fire elsewhere.

Challenged by these questions, this woman experienced such a paradigm shift in her thinking about sexuality that she and her husband never made it to divorce court. She explained, "I'm seventy-two, and I have more intense orgasms now than I've ever had in my whole life!"

I confess I was rather encouraged by this tidbit of information, as I thought, *Hallelujah! Perhaps it only gets better and better as we age.*

God has gifted most of us with a pretty vivid sexual imagination, and that is intended to be a blessing to both our marriage and our marriage bed. We can feel grateful rather than guilty, as long as we are using the sexual energy created within to fuel the home fires, not start a fire elsewhere.

But granted, there are some sexual thoughts that feel far

CELEBRATE THE MENTAL SIDE OF SEX

more like a burden than a blessing—thoughts that awaken all sorts of insecurities and guilt in our minds to the point that our self-esteem and relational confidence erode as naturally as a steep canyon wall. (If this is an issue for you, I encourage you to read *The Fantasy Fallacy: Exposing the Deeper Meaning Behind Sexual Thoughts*.) Most of my coaching clients confess that their sexual thoughts become most problematic when they become directed toward a particular person—a coworker or a friend—rather than simply generic people who don't even exist, except as figments of their own imaginations. In those situations I highly encourage clients to "train their brains" away from such forbidden fruit.

Is that even possible? you wonder. Certainly! We all get to decide what we spend our time thinking about, and we can avoid even pleasurable thoughts about a particular person or activity if we so choose. If I bake a chocolate cake, but want to refrain from eating it until I take it to the person I baked it for, I don't put it on display in the center of my dining table next to a dessert plate and fork. I put it behind a cabinet door or in the pantry. Out of sight, out of mind. If a guy has a weakness for buying fishing gear, but cannot afford to do that right now, he can simply drive right past the Bass Pro Shop on his way home from work. *We* get to decide how much time, attention, and energy we give something. We can choose to "make no provision for the flesh, to fulfill its lusts" (Romans 13:14 NKJV).

Notice that in this passage the Bible's emphasis is on refraining from the *fulfillment* of our lust, not refraining from all sexual thoughts in the first place. Expecting a human being to never think sexual thoughts is like expecting monkeys to never think about bananas or expecting birds not to think about flying. Sorry, but it is never going to happen. The sooner we accept the fact that the human brain is a sexual brain, the better we will be able to control (rather than try to eliminate) our sexual thought patterns.

In the spirit of making no provision for the fulfillment of our lust, here are a few practical things to keep in mind:

- Whatever you fail to feed, eventually, is starved to death, or at least it loses control over you. If there is a particular person that keeps popping up inappropriately in your mind, do not hesitate to simply go out of your way to avoid that person whenever possible.
- If this person seems to be going out of his or her way to be in your presence, make it as un-fun as you can. Stick to business. Don't banter back and forth with innuendos or suggestive comments. Remember that you teach people how to treat you, and you want to be treated with respect for the faithfully married person that you actually are.
- If you are unable to avoid a particular person who seems to be lighting a sexual fire in you, try never to be alone with this person, especially behind a closed door or in a car by yourselves. Many an office romance has started in just such a manner.
- If you must speak privately with this person (a legitimate need, not a justified desire), monitor every word that comes out of your mouth as if your spouse were standing beside you. And keep in mind that nothing is out of God's earshot.
- Refrain from moving conversations to more intimate methods, such as personal phone calls, amorous e-mails, titillating text messages, and the like. No one ever went wrong by keeping things both pure and professional.

- Just because a thought enters your mind or a feeling enters your spirit about a particular person, it *does not* mean you have to act on it. I have thought of robbing a bank many times, but I have never acted on it. And I am not fearful in the least that I ever will, especially considering the harsh consequences. An extramarital affair can certainly yield similar painful and destructive results.
- Remember that thoughts and feelings that are not acted upon cannot possibly hurt you (or your marriage) as badly as those that are.
- As one saying goes, "You can't keep a bird from flying over your head, but you can certainly keep him from building a nest there." In other words, occasional sexual thoughts may be inevitable, but sexual obsessions or actions do not have to result.

Looking back over our relational histories, chances are we have *never* regretted *not* acting out on an inappropriate sexual thought or feeling. Right? Yet if we have acted out at times, regret has most likely come part and parcel soon thereafter. So let's allow history to teach us the valuable lesson of mind-and-mouth control rather than having to learn it anew, shall we?

21. WHAT IS THE HARM IN USING A LITTLE PORNOGRAPHY TO WARM THINGS UP?

One of the couples with whom I have a coaching relationship brought this very question into my office on their first visit. They had been married less than a year, and the husband insisted that one of the things he had anticipated most about being married was having a wife with whom he could watch porn. He saw nothing wrong with the activity as long as there was no secrecy and they were both involved. The only problem with that plan was that his wife *did not* want to be involved and had a big problem with his solo involvement as well.

While I am not proud of this fact, I had a similar dynamic coming into marriage, only in reverse. After we unpacked from the honeymoon, I unpacked my personal little porn collection. *Greg's going to love the fact that I'm willing to watch this with him,* I thought. I thought wrong. He gasped when he saw my handful of VHS tapes, and insisted, "Shannon, get rid of those!"

He went on to explain that he had been addicted to pornography and masturbation as a teenager. As a twenty-six-year-old married man, he had no desire to return to that kind of bondage or to ever have our future children discover such (flesh-covered) skeletons in our closet. The more I thought about his request, the more pleasantly surprised I was. I approached him for a follow-up conversation, just to make sure I understood correctly. "Do you mean to tell me that I . . . *alone* . . . am enough for you? You don't need to look at other women to rev your engine?" I inquired.

"Nope. You're all I need, babe," he confidently replied.

I have never felt more complimented in all my life. In fact, I believe it is one of the reasons I share my body so freely with my husband and with such a happy heart. Even after I've had two pregnancies, forty-six years of aging, and gravity taking its toll, Greg looks at only *my* naked body. I'm "it" for him. He doesn't feel the need to compare; therefore, I don't feel the need to compete. I don't have to. It is "sex the way nature intended" in our bedroom, and we both love it that way.

But not every couple starts their marriage out on such a solid foundation. Somewhere along the way, many of us are naively led astray. "The Bible doesn't specifically mention pornography, so what's the big deal?" many men (and women) want to know. I asked my friend Luke Gilkerson at Covenant Eyes, an Internet accountability and filtering service, about the effects of watching pornography, and he provided not one but five rock-solid answers from his incredibly insightful e-book, *Your Brain on Porn*. He says that watching pornography actually . . .

1. decreases our sexual satisfaction. There is a direct correlation between the amount of pornography viewed and one's overall sexual satisfaction in real relationships. Heavy porn viewers typically report *less* satisfaction with their intimate partners and are less likely to be pleased with their partners' physical appearance, affection, and sexual performance.[1] If porn is actually going to make you experience distaste for your ordained sex partner, how can that be a good thing?
2. disconnects us from real relationships. "The glossy magazine pictures or pixels on the screen have no sexual or relational expectations of their own." This trains [both male and female] viewers to be merely "digital voyeurs," and to "desire the cheap thrill of fantasy over a committed relationship."[2] Our eyes and minds begin to long for something that our hearts and hands can never actually touch. Talk about sexual frustration!
3. lowers our view of women. Rather than men and boys viewing females as beautiful, valuable creatures made in the image of God, most males have unrealistic expectations of

women, often viewing *real* naked women as a far cry from being "porn-worthy."[3] Society obviously pays a high price for this "free porn," particularly women and girls, who feel as if they will never measure up.

4. desensitizes us to cruelty. Even when pornography is considered nonviolent in nature, most of the themes running through the material falsely indoctrinate viewers into the notion that women enjoy acts of aggression and degradation.[4] If we are honest, most pornography should have a label reading: *WARNING: Do Not Try This at Home or She Might Go Ballistic on You!*

5. makes us want to watch more porn. Research findings show that habitual use of pornography leads the viewer to gradually become more tolerant of sexually explicit material. This means he or she must eventually increase the novelty and graphic nature of the material consumed in order to achieve the same level of arousal or interest.[5] We must think of pornography as having the same effect as poison ivy. It is an insatiable itch that only gets stirred up all the more as we attempt to scratch it. The only way to let the rash heal is to refrain from scratching it at all.

Gilkerson explores these findings in much greater detail and goes on to explain the steps required to break free from the bondage of pornography in *Your Brain On Porn*. You might also consider installing the Covenant Eyes Internet filtering software on your home computers, laptops, and smartphones to provide an added level of accountability in your marriage (and to protect your children as well). Installing such software means that you never have to wrestle with the question, "To watch, or not to watch pornography?" The question is answered. The battle is over. The victory is yours. Your integrity is intact. Your marriage and family are protected.

Also, *please* don't wallow in guilt for feeling the pull toward porn in the first place. It is the most common struggle on the planet, so you are certainly not alone. Even the best of Christians face this struggle on a regular basis—from pastors, priests, and school principals to monks and medical missionaries. We all have that temptation looming large over our laptops on occasion.

In fact, 57 percent of pastors say that addiction to pornography is the most sexually damaging issue to their own congregation.[6] So, unfortunately, many Christians are already struggling with the spiritual and relational fallout of having answered the "To watch or not to watch porn?" question incorrectly.

How extensive is the damage? Pornography addictions have robbed many of their marriages, families, finances, careers, self-esteem, and more. Sounds like far too high a price to pay for a pornography-fueled orgasm, doesn't it? I'm thinking there are easier, far less expensive ways to satisfy our healthy sexual cravings within the context of a holy marriage relationship.

Here is what a few of my coaching clients have insightfully concluded about why pornography is such a trap and how we can avoid getting entangled in it:

- William says, "To me, the allure of pornography isn't just the eye candy. It is also the illusion that the woman on the other side is expressing a desire for me. Even though the image is not real, many men fall into this lie because they do not feel the same desire coming from their spouses. My wife wants me . . . to fold the laundry, clean the house, bathe the kids, make money, stop whatever I do that annoys her. The sexy lady on the screen cons me into believing that she wants *me*."

- Elaine says, "It's a complete myth that men want to look at porn and women don't. I'm often tempted to ask my husband to watch something steamy to get my motor running for sex, but what I need isn't looking at other people doing it. I'm simply in need of getting warmed up. Women can't go from zero to one hundred in seconds flat like men can. If a marriage bed is to be kept pure of pornography, there's got to be some intentional foreplay going on so that she has time to get on board the sex train."

- Heath says, "Sex is a relational connector for her but a spiritual protector for him. Because men tend to be drawn toward visual images, our wives play an incredible role in protecting our minds and imaginations from going too far in unhealthy directions (toward other women, especially through pornography). Wives' expressions of sexual desire for us literally protect us from sexual sin. When a wife demonstrates that she has a sexual hunger for her husband, that blows his mind! It also protects him from the lure of other images that offer the same message with no real way to follow through. I wonder if women think of sex in this way. If not, they should."

If the studies and statistics we have mentioned so far are not enough to convince you to steer clear of pornography use, how about simply asking the question, "Where do you want to go?"

One of the first questions a traveler needs to ask in order to get to a destination is, "Where exactly do I want to go?" The same is true in marriage. Is your desired destination intense titillation or intimate relationship? Remember, pornography can drive you to Titillation Station at breakneck speed, but it too often bypasses Relation Station altogether. Think about what your standards are for a healthy sexual relationship, and then answer these questions:

- Is your goal merely more intense orgasms, more novelty, or greater levels of experimentation? Or is it a genuine connection that you both long for?
- Where do you want your spouse's mind to be during lovemaking? Focused on a porn star or on you?
- Could sex actually be *better* if you knew you had *all* of your spouse—not just his or her body but your spouse's full attention?

I believe if husbands and wives are being honest with themselves they would say, "No, I do not want to train my spouse's mind to always need to withdraw into some inappropriate fantasy in order to orgasm. I want to know that he/she is fully present with me."

Also keep in mind that God is the wise designer of sex, and godly sex should not contain elements of lust. (For a refresher course on lust versus love, you might refer back to question 16.) The word *lust* can mean "covet," to crave something that is not yours to have. Luke Gilkerson explains, "Certainly some couples might believe their spouses aren't lusting after the women or men in pornography if they're using it to spice up their bedroom life, but this is turning a blind eye to what's really happening on a mental, emotional, and spiritual level. If your spouse is alone masturbating to porn, he or she is lusting. If your spouse is in the bedroom with you but being turned on by women and men seen on the screen, then your spouse is also lusting. Yes, couples may simultaneously be turned on by their spouses. But this is like eating a salad and washing it down with a Big Mac and saying it was a healthy meal."[7]

PONDER THE PRINCIPLE

- Do we agree that pornography brings more hurt than heat into a marriage relationship? Why or why not?
- Is a porn-free marriage something we aspire to have? If so, what specifically may we need to do to accomplish that goal?

22. WHAT IF I WANT TO TURN A FANTASY INTO A REALITY?

My niece recently had her first baby and is one of the most amazing young moms I have ever seen. She is incredibly attentive and highly protective and rightfully so, considering how much she loves that little girl. She never would want any harm to befall that baby.

So imagine when it comes time for my niece to begin shopping around for a preschool program for her daughter that she is faced with two options. The first option is housed in a facility that is colorful and clean, and the playground has a high fence surrounding it, safely separating the children from any cars or strangers passing by. The second option is equally as eye appealing, and the playground looks like fun, but there is no fence whatsoever. Children are free to wander out into the busy street, and strangers are free to walk right up to students at play.

Is there any question in your mind as to which preschool would be chosen? Of course not. Safety and security are number-one priorities for any concerned parent. Maintaining an impenetrable boundary around such a precious commodity as your child is the first line of defense against the unthinkable.

As a spouse, you need to be equally concerned about maintaining another kind of fence—an impenetrable boundary to protect another deeply cherished relationship, your marriage. When one of my coaching clients tells me that she is considering turning a fantasy into a reality, a red flag always goes up in my spirit. I want to know more—a lot more—about exactly what she has in mind, and, most important, whom else it might involve.

For example, one woman told me that for Valentine's Day she was going to make her husband's fantasy come true by pursuing him in a creative way. She would send him to a nice local hotel, where she would later knock on his door, dressed as a seductive cleaning lady. While not all wives would participate in such an adventurous role play, this scenario seemed tame enough to me to simply applaud her courage and cheer her on. Her husband was both surprised and delighted by the amorous gesture. No harm, no foul.

But another client (I'll call her "Connie") confided that her husband had asked her to arrange a meeting with her old friend from college. When Connie confessed to him that she and her friend had been involved in a rather intimate friendship, wherein lesbian experimentation was involved, he declared her forgiven by himself and by God. But later, aroused by the thought, her husband wanted them to reenact the scenario so he could be a spectator.

I asked Connie how she felt about his request. She sat there in silence, twisting her wedding ring for several seconds. Then, with tears spilling out of the corners of her eyes, she replied, "I struggled with enormous guilt and shame over that situation for years, and it took so much out of me to confess it to him. Initially I was grateful for his compassion and mercy. But to realize that he'd sacrifice my dignity and ask me to re-create such an in-appropriate relationship makes me want to vomit on his shoes and punch him in the stomach! I have to question whether he really loves me at all or if I'm just a sexual object to him." Without a doubt, Connie's husband ripped a scab off of a very deep wound and poured acid on it. Not wise. And he will have a hard time recovering her trust after such a selfish move.

Another couple came to me for marriage coaching after having acted out a fantasy that they initially thought they had gotten away with. Bob and Tina traveled to a convention where they manned a booth together, staying in a posh hotel room both Friday and Saturday night. When Bob suggested they watch porn on his company laptop, Tina was a little reluctant but figured that their teenage children would never know. True, their children never discovered what they had done, but Bob's boss did. The company laptops contained filtering software that sends a report to its IT department whenever any "red flag" activities are suspected. Bob walked into the office Monday morning with a smile on his face from his wild weekend, but he was escorted out the front door with his personal belongings before lunchtime.

Moral of the story? *Some fantasies are far better left as fantasies.* Bringing them to life will often bring far more heartache than heat. So here are some guidelines to help you discern whether to bring a fantasy to life or leave it in your head:

- Does your fantasy involve the presence of any other human being on the planet? Whether the person is a prostitute, porn star, phone sex operator, or personal pal, that is never a good idea. The Bible states clearly and unequivocally that the marriage bed should be kept pure by all (Hebrews 13:4). Translation: only a husband and wife belong there.

- Is the acting out of this fantasy going to cause either spouse to feel used or abused in any way, shape, or form? If so, the resulting pain can never be justified by any amount of derived pleasure.

- If your spiritual leader, boss, or best friend discovered that you had acted out such a fantasy, would it threaten your reputation or your relationship with him or her at all? Equally as important, would it discredit your witness as a follower of Christ?

- Would your job (and livelihood and family security) be in jeopardy if others were to discover this secret part of your sex life?

Let's face it. Political campaigns and budding careers have crumbled. Ministries have imploded and left followers floundering. Families have fallen apart. All because of fantasies that should have never become a reality at all.

So before you decide to turn a fantasy into a reality, be sure to count the potential costs—to your marriage, your ministry, your family, your friendships, your finances, your future reputation. Chances are, keeping that fantasy merely a fantasy is a great safety net against your whole world falling apart.

Dearest Lord, thank You for the incredibly vivid imaginations You have given us. So much of our sexual pleasure is derived from what happens between our two ears, but we need Your help to remain good stewards of that sexual energy. Help us to keep it in check, according to Your will, and to channel it entirely toward the marriage partner You have provided for us. Amen.

Moving Forward Mentally

23. HOW CAN I GET PAST HIS OR HER SEXUAL PAST?

RECENTLY WE WERE TRAVELING DOWN A TWO-LANE HIGHWAY when we approached a blockade stretching from one side to the other. An entire section of the road had collapsed, presumably under the weight of rising floodwaters, and there was no getting over it or going around it. The only option was to back up and find a new route.

A similar dynamic applies to marriage. Sometimes we may discover a mental "roadblock" that seems impossible to simply ignore, and we must figure out a new route to our ultimate destination: genuine intimacy and sexual fulfillment. One of the most common mental roadblocks to intimacy is when one person comes into the marriage with some things in his or her past that may grow bothersome to the other. For example, Don writes via e-mail,

> My wife and I just celebrated our first wedding anniversary. Our sex life has been good, except in one area. I was a virgin when we married. My wife was not, and I knew this. It did not bother me ... until after we said, "I do." I began worrying, *Am I good enough to make her forget? ... Will she compare me? ...*

Will she have flashbacks when we are making love? Will I meet her expectations?

One day she said, "You've never asked me 'how many?'" She followed up with a number that didn't help. It slowly festered, to the point where I began asking questions on my own—and I wish I never had! It only made my fears worse, and even had her remembering things she'd tried to forget!

My question: what do I do when thoughts of her former sex partners come lofting into my mind? The advice so far has been: stop playing tug-of-war with the devil . . . you can't win . . . drop "the rope" (the memories of her lovers). Do you have any extra encouragement or advice?

I am so glad Don asked this question because I certainly do have some strategies for helping one spouse get past the other's sexual past.

FOCUS ON THE POSITIVE, NOT THE NEGATIVE

First think about human nature. When you focus on what you *shouldn't* or *can't* or *won't* allow yourself to think about, guess what you naturally do? You are all the more tempted to think about those very things. Instead, focus on what you *can* or *will* choose to do. There is power in remaining positive. *Choose* to win your spouse's trust (believe me; her insecurities are just as significant as yours), and you will win her heart as well. *Choose* to become her dream lover, which is far more about tenderness than technique, and I guarantee that all previous lovers will pale in comparison.

Want to know *how* to make that kind of healing choice? My husband and I came into our marriage twenty-three years

129

ago with a similar dynamic. He walked into my world a twenty-six-year-old virgin. As for me, between the ages of fifteen and twenty, I had more partners than any woman cares to admit. I forewarned Greg about "what kind of woman" he was interested in before we were engaged. He seemed undaunted. I approached him after two years of marriage crying, "There's no way you could possibly love me if you knew how many men there have been!" yet he remained a rock of stability in my historically unstable world.

> No matter how many sexual partners are in your spouse's past, take comfort and pride in the fact that although you were not the first, you will certainly be the last. No one else can ever love your spouse as you can.

"I don't *need* to know how many, Shannon. But if you *need* to tell me, I'm willing to listen," was Greg's response. I spent a few days combing my memories and creating a long list. It was longer than I had realized it would be. I braced myself for a look of disgust and a renunciation of his wedding vows. As I vocalized the number, I literally choked on the sound of it emitting from my mouth; I was so broken with shame and self-loathing.

"Even if you told me a number one hundred times that, I'm still not going anywhere," Greg firmly replied. "Besides, I know that your past isn't about you and me—it's about you and your dad." Although I didn't understand that at the time, Greg was absolutely right. An emotionally distant father left such a gaping hole in my heart that, as a naive teenager, I went looking for love to fill it. As a result, Greg wasn't the first man I had slept with. But as a result of Greg's unconditional love, I do intend him to be the last. And isn't that what matters most? No matter how many sexual partners are in your spouse's past, take comfort and pride in the fact that although you were not the first, you will certainly be the last. No one else can ever love your spouse as you can.

So for twenty-three years my husband has never even once thrown that number, or my inappropriate past, up in my face. I don't doubt that it has bothered him at times; I cannot imagine how it couldn't. But he has never turned his concerns into ammunition against me, and his commitment to me has not wavered or waffled. We each have tried to focus on overcoming our own issues and insecurities, sharing our thoughts along the way, to build rapport and bring healing rather than getting angry at each other over situations that simply cannot be erased. We have gradually witnessed God do what only God can do—bring deep healing in each of us. This healing has certainly helped both our emotional and sexual confidence, and it has definitely been a win-win.

So my advice to Don, and every other spouse on the planet whose marital partner has a colorful past, "Buck up and be the rock your spouse needs you to be." Don't take your spouse's sexual mistakes personally. It was likely never about you. Be "Jesus with skin on" to him or her. Let your life and love paint a vivid picture of God's unconditional love and mercy. Teach each other that self-worth is not based on a sexual scorecard but on who we are in Christ.

SOME SAFE GUIDELINES TO CONSIDER

A sexually healthy couple is comprised of two sexually healthy individuals, so I encourage you both to be honest about any sexual and emotional baggage that may surface during your lifetime together and be committed to working through it together as a team. By cultivating the fruits of the Spirit from Galatians 5:22–23 (love, joy, peace, patience, kindness, goodness, faithfulness, gentleness, and self-control), couples can forge rich, vibrant marital relationships in the present and future, regardless of what is in their pasts.

Although I feel it is important for spouses to be honest, to a degree, with each other about their sexual histories (particularly histories that involve sexual abuse, addictions, sexually transmitted diseases, pregnancies, and/or abortions—simply because they need to understand the emotional fallout a spouse may experience as a result of these things), I also wholeheartedly believe certain boundary lines should be drawn so *new* trauma is not created during these conversations.

For example, a friend's husband recently confessed his premarital escapades to her, and he was almost cruel with the amount of details he included. In particular, he waxed eloquent about what hotel chain he and his girlfriends typically frequented, and where he preferred to eat breakfast with them the next morning. "Do you have any idea how many Hilton hotels and IHOP restaurants there are in Seattle?" she bitterly inquired of me. I had no idea, but my guess is that she knew exactly how many because that scab was ripped off her wound every time she drove by one of those establishments.

So if confessions need to be made, stick to the *nature* of the sin, but refrain from giving the gory details of the sin, especially details such as (1) the identities of previous sexual partners, (2) specific sexual acts previously engaged in, and (3) specific places where those acts occurred. None of these serve any purpose other than painful reminders of a spouse's sexual misconduct each time that person, place, or thing is encountered or engaged in. Rather than focusing on the who, what, and where of a person's sexual history, focus on the lessons learned during those seasons, what the healing process has looked like since, and how you can support your spouse in his or her continued growth and maturing process.

I know there will be times when these memories will come up, both for you and for your spouse. Simply let those past memories serve as spiritual markers of how far your spouse has come in the journey toward sexual integrity, and celebrate every ounce of progress. Become each other's biggest cheerleader. Discern what you both can learn from those past mistakes; then let those lessons serve your marriage well as you seek to become the sexually and spiritually healthy individuals you both deserve to be.

24. HOW CAN I GET PAST MY OWN SEXUAL PAST?

One particular day Greg and I came across a wedding party while walking on the beach in Australia. The bridesmaids had their dress hems lifted high and were making an elaborate design in the sand with their bare feet by walking around in a huge spiral. The following day I walked past the same area and looked for evidence of their sand art, but it had been erased by the high tide. No traces of it remained—only memories.

At that point I wished every individual and couple who had ever confided in me that they were still struggling with their pasts could have been there with me—women like Felicity, who has had four abortions . . . or Margaret, who wasted eight precious years in an affair with a married man . . . or men like Carson, who lost his job due to looking at porn at work . . . or Evan, who occasionally solicited a prostitute on his lunch hour. Oh, if I had a dime for every person in the world with a past sexual regret, I would be a *very* wealthy woman.

Why did I want to gather all of these previous coaching clients on that beach? For an object lesson. I wanted to say to them: "Whatever we've done in the past, whatever our spouses have done in the past, it's been washed away. The tides of time and God's forgiveness have erased the past, so why do we pretend it's still following us around like our own shadow?"

> If you are still obsessing over your past, know that it is *gone*! Don't let memories of the past haunt you. Don't let yesterday's pain rob you of today's pleasure.

If you are still obsessing over your past, know that it is *gone*! Don't let memories of the past haunt you. Don't let yesterday's pain rob you of today's pleasure. And please understand that not letting the past haunt you does not equate to forgetting the past—the notion that we can "forgive and forget" may be good advice, but it is hard to do when we are the ones who live with the memories of our own mistakes.

As a recovering sex and love addict, I never want to forget where I have been or what I have experienced. Why? It is the best insurance policy against my ever returning to that lifestyle. I want to vividly remember the pain, the shame, the confusion, the desperation. If I don't, it will be too easy to blindly fall back into that pit of sexual and emotional compromise again and again. Someone who has never been burned is far more likely to foolishly play with fire than someone who has been there, done that, and never wants to be burned again.

In addition, I like being able to identify with other people's struggles and empathize with them in a way that few counselors or friends ever could. My graduate degree from the School of Hard Knocks makes me a credible confidant and wise teacher. I dearly love the work I do and the difference I feel it makes in people's lives, marriages, and families. I would not trade my life for anyone else's on the planet, as I have learned that a person's sordid past is often the most direct pathway toward God.

THE BIGGEST QUESTION

I recently spoke to a group of young college women, some married, some single. During a breakout session we conducted an anonymous question-and-answer time where students submitted index cards with whatever questions they would like to ask. After almost twenty years of speaking on the topic of healthy sexuality, nothing really surprises me much anymore, but this question both surprised and blessed me:

> How are you so perky and cheery about life? I mean, you were sexually abused before you were even a teenager, and experienced so many broken sexual relationships before you even finished high school! How can you possibly experience freedom? I feel as if it doesn't exist.

Here is why I am so perky and cheery about life, in spite of the sexual trauma I have experienced and the mistakes I have made: I *know* who I am in Christ.

My biggest question to you, brothers and sisters, is, do you know who *you* are in Christ?

When Jesus died on the cross, He did *not* say, "Forgive them for their sins—except the sexual ones. Those are too big, so I'm not dying for those!" It sounds ridiculous to even consider Jesus saying such a thing, doesn't it? I have absolutely no doubt in my mind that the blood Jesus shed is *more than* enough to cleanse me of every sin I have ever committed and even every sin I will ever commit in the future. That blood is sufficient to cover *all* sin, throughout *all* of history, so why would I think *my* sin is so special that it was surely excluded from His sacrificial act on the cross that day? Absurd. I'm covered. I'm good. I'm free. And that is why I am perky and cheery. Who has the time to be all down about life when we have been given such a miraculous mulligan? We get to start over on any given day because God's mercies are new every morning (Lamentations 3:22–23).

Are you ready to be covered? Good? Free? Perhaps even perky and cheery about life, marriage, and relationships? Then all you need to do is have faith that the blood Jesus shed on the cross is more than enough to cover all of your sin as well. And I can promise you—*it is*! If you are unsure, well, that says a lot more about *you* than it does about God, doesn't it? It really *is* a matter of simply receiving a gift that has already been given, ripping the scarlet letter off our sweaters, and doing a big, fat victory dance because *we are free*! *Woohoo!*

PONDER THE PRINCIPLE

🔥 Is there any sin you have ever committed that Christ excluded from His work on the cross?

🔥 Do you know for certain that you have been cleansed and completely forgiven of anything in your past, or do you still drag around a boatload of guilt? What would it take for you to believe that Christ has redeemed you and removed your guilt completely?

◆ Is there something you want your spouse to stop beating up himself or herself over because it negatively affects his or her self-esteem or your marriage relationship?

◆ If your spouse were to offer you the same clean slate that Christ offers, could you simply receive it and celebrate it?

PASSION PRINCIPLE #3:

Celebrate the Emotional Side of Sex

Moving Beyond Abuse

25. IS IT POSSIBLE TO ENJOY SEX WHEN I HAVE BEEN SEXUALLY ABUSED?

SINCE THE GOAL OF THIS BOOK IS TO CELEBRATE FREEDOM IN THE marriage bed, it may seem odd that I would start this section of the book with themes such as "Moving Beyond Abuse" and "Moving Beyond Betrayal." While abuse and unfaithfulness are certainly nothing worth celebrating, the amazing ability of human beings to heal from these issues and enjoy their sexuality once again certainly is. That is why I have committed so much of my life to helping others recognize the emotional hurdles that hold them back in the bedroom and why I have committed so much time and energy to the counseling process myself.

Yes, I was a victim of sexual abuse. But oddly enough, I didn't even realize it until I was in my late twenties. You may be wondering, "How does one not *know* they were sexually abused as a child?" I'll explain. My first experience with sexual intercourse was with a boy I had been flirting with for all of twenty-four hours. He was eighteen. I was fourteen. Although legally he was an adult and I was a child, this is not the sexual abuse I was referring to. I gave him my virginity willingly.

I had thought about it most of the night before and made a premeditated decision that having sex with him the next day was exactly what I wanted to do. I just didn't understand that the reason I was making such a reckless decision was because of what was going on in a different relationship—in my relationship with my uncle.

I had been invited to stay at my aunt and uncle's apartment for a couple of weeks during the summer, a major relief from the boredom that had set in since my eighth-grade year was completed. I slept in my cousin's bed with her, but on a couple of occasions had been awakened by my uncle in the middle of the night and tugged into the living room. There, he would pull me close to him, forcing his tongue deep into my mouth and groping up and down my backside with his work-worn hands. Each time, I would freeze. I had no idea what to do. If I screamed, it would wake up my aunt or my cousin, and I couldn't stand the thought of either of them discovering what was going on. They were so fond of him. They were so dependent on him. If I messed up their family arrangement, how would they survive without his paycheck? So I did what most girls do in such an awkward position—I did nothing.

As the days passed, these nightly activities grew more intense. Although I was only fourteen, I wasn't stupid. I knew where this was heading. And I knew that I didn't want to give my virginity to my own uncle. He was only related to me by marriage, not by blood, but the thought still seemed so "hillbilly" to me, and it turned my stomach to think of him as being my first.

The next day his son from a previous marriage came to swim at the apartment pool. An incredibly handsome football player much closer to my own age, he seemed like a much better candidate to give my virginity to, so when he made his move the following day, I went through with it. Then, at least if my uncle forced me to have sex with him, I wouldn't be giving him the satisfaction of being the one who had "popped my cherry."

In the end I managed to keep my uncle at bay long enough that my aunt discovered for herself what a lowlife he was, and they divorced shortly thereafter. Unfortunately, there were two other uncles in my life who were trying similar escapades around the same time. One later admitted, "When you started developing breasts and hips, the three of us placed our bets as to which of us would get Shannon in bed first." While none of them succeeded, I later realized through counseling that it was the pressure that each of these men was putting on me that drove me to fling my virginity out the window in a desperate attempt to try to be as "normal" as possible. To me, sex with an eighteen-year-old boy I had just met was the lesser of all those possible evils.

Many of my coaching clients (and perhaps some of you reading this book) have been sexually abused to a far greater degree. I have counseled women who have been forced to have intercourse or oral sex with brothers, sisters, babysitters, youth leaders, fathers, and even mothers. I have known men who were violently sodomized or subtly seduced by male relatives, neighbors, teachers, coaches, fellow athletes, and spiritual leaders. Knowing what I do about how it feels to be taken advantage of by an older, trusted, more powerful figure in your life makes my heart bleed over the pain these people have experienced.

But I do *not* believe for one second that such pain has to totally negate any pleasure we can derive from a healthy sexual relationship with a loving marriage partner. We will talk more about how to invite your spouse into your healing process and enjoy the robust sex life you deserve in questions 26 and 27, but for now I want to ask you just a few seemingly random questions:

- Do you believe that a drama school dropout can become a famous celebrity?
- Do you think that a student cut from a high school basketball team can ever become an NBA all-star?
- Do you think that someone who is fired from a job for lacking imagination or creativity can become one of the most successful entrepreneurs of our day?

We know enough about the human spirit to believe that it is certainly possible to overcome major hardships, setbacks, and challenges, and truly excel at whatever we put our minds to. The drama school dropout I was alluding to in the question above was none other than the late, great Lucille Ball. The basketball player cut by his high school coach? Michael Jordan. The employee fired for lack of original ideas? Walt Disney.[1] These "famous failures" rose above their challenges and eventually got in touch with the true greatness that was woven into the fibers of their being when God created them.

You may think that excelling in drama or sports or business has nothing to do with excelling sexually. I disagree. While we were not all created with a certain gift, knack, or flair for a particular talent or career field, there is one thing that we *all* are created to do well and enjoy. Regardless of whether we are male or female, lily-white or jet-black or some variation in between, regardless of our religious preference, or whether we came from a rich or poor neighborhood, it is in us all to be *sexual* beings. It is our main common denominator, and there is no erasing or ignoring it.

Perhaps your earliest experiences with your sexuality were negative, guilt inducing, shame based, or maybe even extremely traumatic. You might have felt tempted in the past to believe that you have been scarred permanently and are broken beyond repair—that you simply are not *sexual* anymore as a result. While I want to be sympathetic to your pain, I will never agree with that assessment. Why? I know for certain that there is absolutely *no* wound our Savior cannot work wonders on. There is simply no abuse He does not have a healing balm for. He has a miracle for every malady we humans experience, and I wholeheartedly believe He can bind up every heart that has been broken—even those that have been broken because of sexual abuse.

Not only can He alleviate your pain; He can even help you tap into and fully enjoy the sexual passion and pleasure both you and your spouse were originally designed to experience. If that sounds like something you are ready to receive, then keep reading as we discuss how marriage can actually be the relationship that brings such welcome relief.

26. SHOULD I TELL MY SPOUSE ABOUT THE ABUSE OR KEEP IT TO MYSELF?

In my late twenties I went through six months of intense group and individual counseling, wrestling with the question, *why— as a happily married woman in youth ministry—do I still wrestle with the overwhelming temptation to look for love in extramarital relationships?*

As my counselor helped me lift the rug I had been sporting in the living room of my life, we recognized big piles of guilt and shame I had gingerly swept underneath, hoping no one would ever be wise to what had happened to me during those pivotal pubescent years—the sexual abuse from my uncles, the surrender of my virginity to a practical stranger, and the resulting promiscuity and multitude of sexual partners that littered my teenage years. Proverbs 26:11 tells us that a fool returns to his folly as a dog returns to his vomit, and I was doing just that—still longing to find my self-esteem in the arms of yet another man (because that seemed to be where I had lost it in the first place). It was usually with an older man in some form of authority over me, a clue that told me I was still in search of a father figure, to medicate my emotional pain from the distance in my relationship with my own dad.

As I learned more and more about what I had come to understand was a form of "sex and love addiction" for me, I knew I couldn't keep these revelations to myself. I had to let Greg in on my dirty little secrets—*all* of them. He knew about my promiscuous teen years, but I had never told him how that snowball got started rolling downhill. I had never told him about my uncles.

When I searched my heart as to why I hadn't told him, even after seven years of marriage, I realized that the guilt and shame had stuck with me like a wad of bubblegum on the sole of my shoe. Deep down, I feared that if Greg knew I had been physically involved with male relatives, surely he would view me as "damaged goods" and want a refund on the relational commitment he had made. But after seven years of silence, I could not hide behind the happy mask any longer. Through a torrent of tears, one night I told him everything. And his response built a bridge between where I had been stuck for years and where I longed to be emotionally and sexually.

I will tell you more about that healing experience in response to the next question and how you can be a healing force in your spouse's life as well. But for now I want to tell you several reasons why it was so important for me to discuss my abuse with my spouse and why I believe every married couple should have similar conversations about whatever abuses may be in their own pasts.

First, to verbalize out loud exactly what happened to me between the ages of twelve and fourteen helped me realize that my uncles were the abusers. *I* was not a "willing participant," as I had originally assumed, but a paralyzed victim. They were adults, and I was merely a child—a child who hadn't been taught the assertiveness skills to get herself out of an uncomfortable and compromising situation. I was not to blame, so I could let go of any sense of guilt. No court of law would have held a junior high girl responsible for the actions that took place. So if I wasn't *guilty*, I could conclude I was *innocent*.

Lesson #1: Whatever abuse you have experienced was not *your fault. You are not a guilty party. You were an innocent victim, and mature adults (such as your counselor or spouse) will confirm that to be true.*

So if I was innocent, why was I feeling so much shame? I came to understand that shame is like a hot potato. It gets tossed around in the dysfunctional dance of sexual abuse, and when the abuser refuses to hold it, the victim usually winds up feeling stuck with it. So I decided to literally take my hands and "scoop out" all the shame I had been carrying around in my soul for the past fifteen years. Then, upon my counselor's invitation, I symbolically dumped it all into her trash can, which seemed like a much more appropriate place for such infectious garbage than inside my spirit. That moment left me feeling fifty pounds lighter and opened the doorway to a much healthier sexual identity.

Lesson #2: We don't have to hold on to the hot potato of shame. We can choose to let it go. There are better places for it than inside our souls, and removing it simply makes room for better things, such as peace, joy, and contentment.

Next, I needed to reestablish a sense of self-esteem. I contemplated what a human being is worth, in spite of any sexual abuse he or she has experienced. I thought about how the word *abuse* means that something has experienced "ab(normal)use." It has been inappropriately used for a purpose for which it was not created. But does that lessen its value?

If my son uses my grandmother's china plate to cover the bathtub drain, does that mean it can no longer decorate my holiday table and serve my guests delightful food? Of course not. If my daughter uses my lipstick to paint a mural on her bedroom window, does that mean it can no longer tint my lips before I go out in public? No. When I asked myself, "If my uncles touched me in ways that they shouldn't have, does that mean I can't enjoy my husband touching me in ways that are perfectly appropriate, comforting, and even arousing?" The answer, of course, was *no.* No! NO! My uncles may have robbed me of my dignity and sexual self-esteem long ago, but I resolved I would *never* let that happen again—not on any given day, not ever.

Lesson #3: Simply because one person has treated you in a sexually inappropriate way doesn't lessen your value as a sexual human being. You can still enjoy being treated in a sexually appropriate way by the spouse who has committed his life and love to you.

As you embrace and celebrate these three valuable life lessons—(1) that you are in no way guilty of being abused as a child, (2) that you can let go of any sense of shame, and (3) that you are still a valuable sexual being—you will feel a seismic shift in your spirit. You will learn to trust that your spouse is *not* your abuser, and you no longer will feel the need to guard yourself or to punish your spouse for the sexual baggage you have been dragging around. You will be able to recognize your mate as a safe partner who is fully invested in your healing process, and you will begin to feel more comfortable in your own skin as you share what has been going on inside you for so long in response to what you experienced in childhood.

> The very sexual acts or sensations that have brought you great pain in the past can eventually become a source of great pleasure. You *can* retrain your brain to accept and celebrate the healthy sexual energies flowing between you and your mate.

Believe it or not, the very sexual acts or sensations that have brought you great pain in the past can eventually become a source of great pleasure. You *can* retrain your brain to accept and celebrate the healthy sexual energies flowing between you and your mate. And when that happens, you no longer will feel like a victim but will instead feel like a victor.

So set the stage for your own personal victory over any sexual abuse in your past, and prepare to share your deepest self—the good, the bad, and the ugly—with the one person on the planet who holds the most power to help you heal.

PONDER THE PRINCIPLE

🌢 Why do you think it may be so difficult for victims of sexual abuse to be honest about what they have experienced?

⚬ Although being sexually abused may negatively affect people's self-esteem, does it make them any less valuable as human beings? Why or why not?

⚬ What are some things you can think of that would help people heal from sexual traumas?

27. HOW CAN I HELP MY SPOUSE HEAL FROM THE SEXUAL ABUSES HE OR SHE SUFFERED?

Revisiting the painful but incredibly cathartic conversation I had with Greg during my season of counseling, I have recognized multiple things that he did in response that spoke volumes to me about what a safe relationship our marriage actually was. I want to share those things with you, to encourage you in becoming a "soft place for your partner to land" as he or she lets down his or her guard and learns to sift through the ashes of any sexually abusive experiences.

1. *Listen to the story.* You may be worried that you are not a trained counselor or that you won't know what to say in response. It's okay. Just because your spouse decides to share something scary from the past does not mean he or she is expecting you to *fix* or *heal* him or her. It is simply such a relief to take off your mask and be real with someone, and what better someone to be real with than your own husband or wife?

2. *Pay attention to your body language.* I will never forget the first counselor I went to for help with my past. As I began unpacking my sexual baggage, she began to squirm,

shifting from one side of her chair to the other, crossing and uncrossing her legs repeatedly, glancing up on occasion with a look of horror on her face, perhaps as a way of showing empathy, but I couldn't be sure. She scribbled a lot of notes and made very little eye contact. I left her office feeling heavier than when I had come in. I felt judged and concluded from her uncomfortable responses that I was a hopeless case.

Greg, on the other hand, was everything I needed a listening ear to be. He looked directly into my eyes and listened patiently, only taking mental notes—questions he wanted to ask for clarification to make sure he understood me correctly. He constantly caressed my hand or knee, which I interpreted as, "I'm here for you, babe. It's okay. Keep going." So I did. I told him everything I could remember. And I felt as if a two-ton dump truck full of emotional garbage finally vacated my mental property.

3. *Legitimize the pain.* Greg easily could have said, "Well, at least your uncles never succeeded in having sex with you," or "I don't understand why you've never told someone," or some other minimizing statement. But instead, he replied with something along the lines of, "I can't imagine how that must have made you feel to be treated that way at such a young age. I'm so sorry that you experienced that, and that you've never felt safe enough to tell anyone." Most sexual abuse victims have questioned their own right to whatever emotions they have experienced, and they often just need someone to tell them that they are not crazy or overreacting.

4. *Keep your own emotions in check.* After speaking to an audience of youth pastors and their wives about dealing with teens who have been sexually abused, I was approached by a couple asking for a quick private conversation. After my talk the wife decided to disclose for the first time to her husband that she had been sexually abused by a close relative. Unfortunately the husband's response was that he was ready to leave the conference, track down the relative, and beat him to a pulp. The look on his wife's face said, loud and clear, "I wish I'd never told him now!" But a cat like that won't go back into the bag once you let it out. So I sat them both down and asked the wife, "Is this the response you wanted from your husband?" to which she replied, "No! I forgave the guy years ago, and I don't want to dig it all back up!"

The husband fumed and punched a clenched fist into his other flat hand over and over, trying to contain his rage. I told him, "She doesn't need you to be mad at him. She needs you to be sad for her. That's all." Tears began to spill from his eyes and stream down his cheeks, as if all he needed was permission to open his floodgate of sadness over the situation. After a few sobs he was able to pull himself together, then pull her close to him. Rather than swearing to kill the guy, he apologized for both his aggressive response and for the pain she had endured.

No doubt, whatever abuse your spouse experienced as a child, you are going to feel a great deal of pain for him or her. But stealing the spotlight and focusing on your own emotions too heavily is not nearly as therapeutic as responding to his or her pain first and foremost, and then soon thereafter you can process your own pain.

5. *Ask clarifying questions.* As I was telling Greg about the details of my experiences, he was connecting dots in his mind. After hearing how nauseating it was to be kissed by a man who tasted like an ashtray, Greg inquired, "Is that why you get so mad when people smoke around you?" I had never given it much thought but realized that surely there must be a connection. His radar also went off when I described how painful it was to have my uncle's bristly mustache boring into my tender upper lip, and he asked, "Is that why you don't kiss me nearly as often since I grew a mustache?" Again, it wasn't a conscious choice, but I had to agree that I liked the feel of a smooth face much better. The next morning Greg was fervently shaving off all his facial hair and had called in late to work so he could stay home and catch up on months of missed kisses. After fearing that he would think I was damaged goods, that decision on his part was incredibly healing for me.

6. *Allow sexual boundaries to be reestablished.* Think of what a child experiences when he or she has been sexually abused, and then fast-forward the tape of that life ten, twenty, or thirty years. What do you often have? A scared little girl or boy trapped in a grown person's body, often in a marriage that suffers sexually because of ghosts from the past that have never been confronted.

As I explained to my counselor what my uncles attempted with me and how, she inquired, "Tell me about your sex life with your husband." I admitted that I wasn't the most sexually interested person in the world. Most attention or affection Greg showed toward me I misinterpreted as, "You just want sex." My response was often, "Well, forget it," because, subconsciously, it just felt too much like I was being sexually abused all over again. Only this time it was supposed to be okay. But it wasn't. There was very little in me that ever really wanted, craved, or deeply desired sex with my husband. And this was a problem, more so in his mind than in my own.

My counselor drew a stick figure on a chalkboard with a big circle around it. Then she took an eraser and turned the solid circle into a perforated one. She explained how every person is born with a natural boundary around him that allows him to feel safe in the presence of others. But when that boundary is broken by someone who seeks to touch you against your will, either violently or sexually, you never feel completely safe again until that boundary is completely reestablished.

But I wondered, *How do you reestablish your own personal sexual boundaries when you're already married?* So I asked. And she answered me with a question: "What would happen if you told your husband that you needed a designated period of time where sex is not an expectation whatsoever?" I thought, *Yeah . . . that will go over like a lead balloon.*

7. *Accept* no *as a sign of healing.* Greg somehow understood the logic of what my counselor was suggesting. Until I felt complete freedom to say *no* to sex, I would never feel complete freedom to say a wholehearted *yes* to sex. He asked, "How long do you think you'll need?" I asked for two months. He agreed.

8. *Celebrate* yes *as a sign of success.* The simple fact that Greg was so willing to become a fully invested partner in my

healing process (even to the degree of going without sex for two whole months) melted my heart toward him. And within two weeks I was literally *begging* him to make love to me. Thinking I had failed my counseling homework, I confessed at my next appointment. My counselor simply smiled and replied, "You didn't fail. You accomplished exactly what you needed. Just a little faster than you expected."

9. *Be sensitive to triggers.* As a general rule, I have felt incredibly safe having sex with my husband ever since that season of counseling. But there have been a few times when Greg did or said something that sent me reeling with fear or anger. He has learned that he should *never* (1) sneak up on Shannon and grab any body part when she isn't expecting it, (2) wake her up in the middle of the night from a dead sleep by touching her sexually, and (3) tickle or poke her relentlessly and say, "Cry Uncle!" to get him to stop. Any of those things may get him punched, and now he completely understands why.

10. *Be Jesus with skin on.* The most important thing that any spouse can do is demonstrate to the other person the same response that Jesus would. Sentiments such as:

- You are loved. Period. No conditions or exceptions.
- You are safe. Someone else may have used or abused you, but I never will.
- You are valuable. You do not mean less to me because of any brokenness or pain you bring to the table. I celebrate *all* of you—the good and the bad.
- Our relationship is a healing place. You can tell me anything, and your secrets are safe with me.

- My arms and my heart are always open to you.
- You don't have to look any further for acceptance.
  I accept you fully for who you are—nothing more,
  nothing less.

Helping your spouse heal from any sexual abuse he or she experienced in childhood may be one of the most valuable ministry opportunities of your life, so let's pray for success in that endeavor.

Lord Jesus, only You know how prevalent sexual abuse is in our society and how deeply it wounds a human being, male or female, to be used by a trusted adult in a way that You never intended. You also know what kind of burden past sexual abuse can place on a marriage relationship and on a marriage bed in particular. We ask that You would do what only You can do, God. Bring complete healing to every heart that's experienced such pain and confusion. Help each victim overcome his or her resulting fear of intimacy and feelings of low self-esteem, anger, and bitterness. Give marriage partners wisdom and insight as to how to be a healing force in their spouses' lives. Restore every joy and pleasure to marriage beds, and show us how to minister to our spouses through the sacred gift of genuine intimacy. Amen.

Moving Beyond Betrayal

28. WHAT IF I FIND IT DIFFICULT TO TRUST MY SPOUSE?

I NEVER WILL FORGET THE SOUND OF UNCONTROLLABLE SOBBING over the telephone as I talked with Tonya about the many ways she was driving her husband (and herself) nuts. She would intercept every magazine that came in the mail and cut out every picture of any woman whom she perceived as even possibly "prettier" than her. When I asked her why she felt that need, at first her reply was, "Isn't it my responsibility to keep my husband from lusting after other women?"

"No, Tonya, it's not *your* responsibility. You can't control anyone but yourself, and your husband can't be controlled by anyone other than himself. You realize that, right?" I inquired.

"I guess, but I still feel as if I have to control his environment. When we're at dinner parties, if he leaves the table to go to the bathroom, I go to the bathroom, too, just in case there is some other woman along the way who wants to try to talk to him," she confessed.

"How does your husband feel about your following him to the bathroom?" I asked.

Tonya admitted that it probably drives him crazy, and that

the fact she would even feel the need to do such a thing drove her crazy too. We talked quite a while longer about the great lengths she would go to in order to "control his environment." Basically, this guy didn't make a move without his wife knowing about it. And both were panicked over what it might mean if any of her suspicions were ever confirmed.

"Have you ever heard of a 'self-fulfilling prophecy,' Tonya?" I asked, going on to explain that sometimes *we* create the very behavior in someone else that we are trying so desperately to control, simply by being so controlling. When people get the message loud and clear, "I don't trust you. I *can't* trust you!" then guess what? They begin to believe it themselves. They are brainwashed by their own spouses into thinking, "I'm untrustworthy." So then they simply act in accordance with what they believe about themselves. We can create the very unstable relationship that we fear most—all because of our own insecurities.

Truth be told, I have talked with numerous Tonyas in my life-coaching practice, as well as many "Toms" (the male version). Their tactics have included . . .

- forcing their spouses to go to counseling in spite of their unwillingness to do so, sometimes to deal with issues that exist only in their own heads
- following their spouses' cars to see if their spouses go where they said they were going after work
- stalking Facebook pages, text messages, e-mails, and so forth
- privately asking their spouses' coworkers to comment on their spouses' office behavior
- enlisting friends to spy on or even flirt with their spouses just to see how they respond

My best advice to anyone who feels compelled to go to such great lengths to follow up on a spouse's faithfulness or set a trap to catch him or her in the act—professional help is definitely needed; but *you* may be more in need of it than your spouse! If you discover that there *is* an issue that warrants concern, I hope you *both* will get counseling, rather than just expecting your spouse to deal with his or her issue alone. It takes two to tango in any dysfunctional relationship dance.

As Tonya and I dug a little deeper into where her extreme insecurities may have originated, she realized it was probably because she grew up knowing a secret that no one else in her family was privy to—her grandfather had been sexually unfaithful to her grandmother, and Tonya's biggest fear was becoming her grandmother—someone whose husband was unfaithful. When I asked Tonya exactly how she learned of her grandfather's infidelities, she admitted something she had never told anyone. She knew for a fact that her grandfather had cheated on her grandmother because he had cheated . . . with *her.*

Suddenly it all made a lot more sense. Tonya had layers and layers of sexual trauma that she never had worked through. Not only did she fear becoming her grandmother if her husband was unfaithful, but she also was panic-stricken that if her husband ever found out what had happened to her as a young girl, he surely would not feel sexually attracted to her anymore. And this would greatly increase the chances of his being sexually attracted to someone else. As much as Tonya has a right to her feelings of insecurity due to experiencing something no child should ever have to experience, her husband also has some rights. There is a reason why a person is "innocent until proven guilty" in the United States, but such wasn't the case in Tonya's world. She was declaring her husband *guilty* and exacting the price of extreme accountability that her grandfather owed.

Speaking of extreme accountability, I am not saying it is never called for, and we will discuss it more in the next question. But unless he or she has already shattered your trust in the past, you owe your spouse the benefit of the doubt. What might that look like? I make some coaching clients' toenails curl when I explain the long leash that I am on in my own marriage (versus the short leash that some spouses experience). The motto my trusting husband of twenty-three years lives by is, "I'm going to give you enough rope to hang yourself or tie a bow with it." In other words, he gives me all the freedom in the world (within reason) to make my own choices: for example, when or how often I call to check in, whether to talk to the stranger next to me on the airplane, whether to take a travel companion with me to a certain event, or how many days of the year to travel. He feels no need to control me. He doesn't want to control me. He prefers that I simply control myself. So I do, and it is in no way difficult. I know that Greg believes in me, so I am *internally* motivated to live up to or even exceed his expectations. And internal motivation is a lot more effective than any external factors.

Yes, Greg feels this much trust in me despite the fact that I have done some pretty untrustworthy things in the earlier years of our marriage. When I asked him one day where he finds the courage to give me as much freedom as he does, he replied, "I realized a long time ago that if you were going to cheat on me, there'd be nothing I could do to stop you, so it seemed best to simply relax and not stress about it, as crazy as that sounds. But it's a strategy that's worked beautifully. I've given you the choice every day to be with me, or with someone else, and you're still here, so I figure I must be doing something right by not hovering over you."

I offer Greg the same courtesy, of course. I have never lost one minute of sleep over where he may be, who he may be with, or anything he may be doing. I assume that if he thinks I should be aware of a potential stumbling block in his path, he will call it to my attention, and I will gladly hold him accountable with love and respect. But I do not obsess over petty stuff, such as what is on his Facebook page or who texted him today or what he may think of the attractive office secretary. It is simply not on my radar.

Marlene has experienced both extremes—being externally motivated by a controlling husband and being internally motivated, thanks to a trusting husband. She shares these words of warning and encouragement:

> I've traveled for business on a regular basis for the last twelve years. The first five of those years I was in a controlling, manipulative marriage; I was expected to phone at a certain time each day, and my suitcase was scrutinized to see what I was packing and if I had a bathing suit with me. I would do laps in the hotel's pool, but the interpretation was that I was trolling for men. I was grilled on who I met with, whether they were male or female, what I wore . . . you get the idea.
>
> The behavior certainly didn't motivate me to honor his demands and, in fact, did become a self-fulfilling proph-ecy, eventually leading me into an extramarital affair. Don't misunderstand—I'm not saying my husband's actions were responsible for my affair. Clearly that was a choice I made myself, out of low self-esteem and a need to find affirmation. I

contrast those first five years with the past two years since I've remarried, and I'm so grateful that my new husband gives me the benefit of the doubt. I'm highly motivated to let him know I arrived safely somewhere and to text him throughout the day to let him know how things are going. He trusts me completely, and as a result, I respond in kind and honor his trust. The responses the two different behaviors elicit are night and day. Everyone needs to understand that negative actions result in negative responses.

Do you have this kind of unwavering trust in your marriage, or might there be some "self-fulfilling prophecies" in the making? If the latter is a truer statement, what do you think your own relational insecurities communicate to your mate—(1) I have enough self-esteem to expect my spouse to be fully committed to me, *or* (2) I have such low self-esteem that I automatically assume that no one would ever be faithful to someone like me? Your answer to that question will most likely reveal a lot more about yourself than it does about your spouse.

Before you let your own personal insecurities ooze out and ruin the very fibers of your relational rug, consider taking the high road. See if you are able to make the following declarations to your spouse:

- I believe in you 100 percent, and I trust you completely.
- Although you are a fallible human being, I know your conscience will be your guide. I trust you have the Holy Spirit guiding you.
- I don't feel the need to go behind your back to check up on you, and that feels really good.

- If I have any concerns about your marital faithfulness, I will simply ask you, with complete confidence that you will be honest with me.
- As we continue putting all of our emotional eggs in each other's baskets from day to day, I have no doubt that you will treat my heart as carefully as I will treat yours.

Set the standard high as to what you expect from both yourself and your spouse, and then live up to it and believe that your husband or wife will do the same. That way, insecurities won't have a chance to develop or fester.

Always remember that a person is innocent until proven guilty, and keep your personal insecurities in check as *your own* issues to deal with, rather than turning the tables and letting them evolve into relational poison. And as you put this kind of stock in your spouse's character and integrity, I believe it will yield a tremendous amount of compound interest. Your spouse will undoubtedly want to rise to the occasion and prove incredibly worthy of your trust.

29. CAN MARITAL TRUST BE REESTABLISHED WHEN BROKEN? IF NOT, IS DIVORCE AN OPTION?

Unfortunately not all suspicions of a spouse's unfaithfulness are completely unfounded or based on our own insecurities, as we just discussed. Sometimes that nagging feeling inside one's gut— the one that is absolutely impossible to ignore—really is the Holy Spirit prompting you to take action. And when you take action, ask the hard questions, discover disheartening bitter truths, and are forced to face your alternatives, you most likely will experience some of the darkest, most challenging days of your existence. If you are "that husband" or "that wife" right now, I am so sorry you are on this painful path.

I acknowledge that sometimes divorce *is* the only way a marriage can find relief from repeated affairs or sexual addictions. The unfaithful party must take responsibility, seek counseling to get to the root causes of the infidelities, and begin earning trust back one day at a time. If he or she refuses to do that, the offended party might feel the need to exercise "tough love" (as Dr. James Dobson explains in his book *Love Must Be Tough*), drawing firm boundary lines to protect himself or herself from a spouse whose guilt is unquestionable.

The Bible does allow divorce as one acceptable way of relieving the enormous stress that comes from being married to someone who chooses to be unfaithful (Matthew 5:31–32; Matthew 19:3–9). Hopefully this book will prevent either of you from ever falling into a pattern of unrepentant adultery and give you the tools you need to rebuild the broken parts of your relationship before things descend to that level of discord.

Of course, some spouses declare that even in the face of marital infidelity, they are simply not ready to jump ship, throw in the towel, or raise the white flag. Instead, they hunker down and fight for their marriage like never before. The rest of this section is for those who choose to fight.

Although we cannot play "God" or the Holy Spirit in the lives of unfaithful spouses, we can be used as holy instruments to "bring down their house of cards." We can ask that they make themselves accountable and communicate honestly about their daily interactions until confidence in marital faithfulness is restored. Then a

real relationship can be built on a much more secure foundation—
one built on gut-level honesty and integrity rather than bald-faced
lies and compromise.

My friends Steve and Holly Holladay know firsthand what
that rebuilding process is like. They are cofounders of Ultimate
Escape (www.ultimateescape.org), a ministry that helps young
people pursue healthy sexuality. Married for twenty-four years
and a father of four, Steve is a certified pastoral sexual addiction
specialist, whose main goal is to help young people steer clear of,
or break free from, the sexually destructive lifestyles that kept
him in bondage for so many years.

When Steve admitted to Holly his (mental) sexual addiction,
she says she tasted bile. She could not believe what she was hearing and could not fathom that their marriage could ever survive.
But through many years of counseling, honest conversations, and
gut-wrenching prayers for God's guidance, their marriage is not
just surviving—it is actually thriving. Holly's restoration process
is detailed on her blog,[1] but for the purpose of this book, she has
three tidbits of advice (applicable to both women and men) that
will hopefully help you survive the storm of marital unfaithfulness if it ever blows into your hometown. Holly writes:

1. YOU DON'T NEED TO KNOW EVERYTHING!

As Steve disclosed his history of sex addiction to me,
curiosity threatened to ruin us. I wanted to know everything.
Everything! While his addiction had not physically involved
another person, mentally it had involved many. And I wanted
to know the details about every single one. Who were these
women who occupied my husband's head? Did I go to church
with them? Were they prettier and skinnier than me? Were

they my friends? These kinds of questions took up all the space in my head, leaving room for nothing else.

When any addiction is being addressed in marriage, disclosure is vital. Sharing every gory detail is not! In simple terms, disclosure is stating facts, sharing secrets, coming clean, and telling the basic history of the addiction. Because addictions are often seeded in secrecy and dishonesty, it is important to get everything out in the open and work from there. Honest disclosure is how you start rebuilding trust.

At first, I confused disclosure with knowing every detail. Initially, Steve's reluctance to share the details with me hurt. I saw it as a way for him to continue being dishonest. We had to sort out how to deal with this difference of opinion before we could start repairing our relationship.

I had to decide which was more important—knowing everything or knowing enough. Knowing enough meant I knew the important things: that Steve had been honest with me and was committed to becoming authentic in our relationship. Knowing enough didn't threaten to do more damage to our marriage. Knowing everything would have. There is a place for telling every detail, but it's not with your spouse. The best place for that kind of sharing is with an accountability partner or counselor, with someone who is healthy and safe. If Steve had given in and shared the sordid details with me, it would have hindered the healing of our relationship.

So when a betrayed husband or wife asks me if they need to know everything, my answer is no. Over a decade later, I am thankful that Steve didn't give in and share too many details with me. Now I don't have to battle images that were never meant to be in my mind. Being out of the loop allows both of us the freedom to have a clear mind when we interact. Now we are free to live in the present, free from the ghosts of the past.

2. DON'T CREATE HIGHER STANDARDS THAN WHAT YOU CAN LIVE UP TO YOURSELF.

When we enter into a committed relationship, there are some basic expectations that come with the territory—one of the most primal being that we will be the sole object of our partner's desire. It is innate. We long to be desired. And we don't expect to share that position with anyone else. I never expected to be one of many women who floated through my husband's mind. In reality, over the course of Steve's active addiction, I was one of thousands. I wanted to be the only one.

Walking the road of recovery with Steve, I have learned that wanting to be the only one is fine. Actually being the only one is unrealistic. In marriage it is fair to expect faithfulness—emotionally, physically, and mentally. But expecting that Steve will never have some image flip through his head is unfair. So the real issue becomes the intent.

In an active addiction, there is a complete lack of emotional intimacy between partners. An addict will attempt to fill this void by pursuing false intimacy with someone else— real and/or fantasy. The intent is to use images or people for one's own pleasure. It is selfish in nature and it is wrong. But if I'm honest, I have to admit that while I have never struggled with a sexual addiction, sometimes there are uninvited thoughts and images that appear in my own head. How can I hold my partner to a standard that I, myself, can't keep?

So if you value your relationship and want to heal it, it is better to focus on what you can do to cheer your spouse on and turn his or her heart (and thoughts) back toward you, rather than berate him with a bunch of questions that can't really be answered in a futile attempt to calm your own insecurities. Because in reality, there will never be a way to know who is in your spouse's head as he or she is kissing you. But build emotional intimacy, and it won't matter. You'll know your spouse's heart and body belong to you even if another unwelcome individual invades his or her private thoughts on occasion.

3. YOU CAN FORGIVE, ALTHOUGH YOU'LL MOST LIKELY NEVER FORGET.

When you hear the phrase "forgive and forget," I suspect you think it means to literally forgive and never think about, remember, obsess over, or plot revenge about said incident ever again. Ever! Or at least that was the understanding I used to have. Why on earth did I ever put that much pressure on myself? It is literally impossible not to remember, especially when it involves hurts inflicted by a spouse. Telling yourself not to remember is like trying not to stick your tongue in the hole where a tooth used to be. The harder you try not to, the more you do it.

Life experience has taught me that forgiveness is a choice. It's something I choose even when I don't feel like it. And it's a choice that has to be made over and over. It is a process— not an event. It's much like the decision to lose weight. When people decide to lose weight, they aren't successful by making a one-time decision. It takes lots of decisions every day to be successful; eat this, don't eat that, go to the gym. And, like choosing forgiveness, decisions regarding lasting weight loss are made over and over, day after day.

Over time, as I have continually chosen to forgive, I have been set free. And oddly enough, I have even been freed from seeing the hurts in a purely negative light. The more time that passes and the stronger the relationship becomes, I find myself seeing those very hurts as a blessing in disguise. Remembering allows me to see how far we have come. If you have chosen to forgive, know that you will remember from time to time. When you do, give yourself permission to feel whatever you feel in that moment; name it and move on. Then make the choice yet again to forgive and forget, at least until you remember it again.

The key to overcoming any sense of betrayal and broken-ness *is* forgiveness. And I have witnessed many spouses make that tough but tender choice to forgive, such as . . .

- Doug, who upon hearing his wife's tearful confession of a sexual affair she had blindly stumbled into, escorted her into their bathroom, filled the tub with warm water, and immersed her trembling body as a symbol of his unconditional love and desire for her sexual and spiritual healing.
- Stacy, who after discovering her husband's pornography addiction, chose not to throw a stone but to throw herself completely into couple's counseling to learn more about the emotional triggers that sent him spiraling. By God's grace, she was able to look past his weaknesses and recognize his genuine needs for acceptance, approval, and affirmation.

I have also seen the offending spouse go to great lengths to earn trust once again, such as . . .

- Bobby, who went to an Every Man's Battle workshop to deal with his sexual addiction and came completely clean with an accountability partner with whom he meets each week. He also installed an application on his mobile phone that lets his wife know his exact whereabouts at all times. (You can learn more about the Every Man's Battle workshops at www.newlife.com.)
- Julia, who asked her husband's permission to quit her high-level, high-paying job to escape an extramarital emotional entanglement with a fellow coworker. "I knew it would be too dangerous to keep sticking my head in that lion's mouth day after day, so I chose to leave the lion's den altogether," she says. And true to His form, God provided a great new job soon thereafter.

There are so many practical ways spouses can show that they really are serious about rebuilding trust and genuine intimacy in the relationship, so discuss those together (with a counselor if necessary) and come up with a game plan for victory. In the words of Sarah Palin, "Don't retreat! Reload!" Marriages are worth fighting for!

And keep in mind that when devastating disappointments arise, you really have only two choices. You can choose a Bitter Land, where wounds are left gaping for decades, where resentments alter personalities and unresolved anger etches deep lines in both your face and your soul. Or you can choose a Better Land, where broken hearts are bound and healed, where resentments gradually fade like the morning fog, and where a great sense of victory and joy takes up residence in every fiber of your being because of what you have allowed God to do in your marriage. In the next question you will hear more about how Steve and Holly chose that Better Land and how you can do the same.

Dear God, it can be so difficult to understand the extramarital temptations that creep in and even more difficult to forgive our spouses when they let those temptations get the best of them. But we thank You for the example that You set for us on the cross. Give us the same spirit of mercy and compassion so the kindness and unconditional love we show our spouses will lead to genuine repentance whenever necessary. In Jesus' name we pray, amen.

Evolution of a Relationship

30. WHAT IF MY HEART IS TELLING ME THAT I MARRIED THE WRONG PERSON?

WHEN MY CHILDREN WERE MUCH YOUNGER, THEY WOULD OFTEN come home from school spouting all kinds of information about who did what to whom, for what reason, the resulting consequences, other people's responses to those consequences, and on and on. Knowing that kids are very capable of spinning quite colorful tales, I usually felt the need to ask, "And how do you know all of this?" Sometimes the source was quite credible, such as a teacher or other parent. Other times—say, if the story came from another child—I would have to explain that before you believe anything, you must always "consider the source."

The source of any information must always be considered, even if that information is coming from inside our own selves. When people say, "My heart is telling me . . ." a red flag usually starts waving in my mind. As a life coach, I want to start asking all kinds of clarifying questions to make sure that their hearts are not about to mislead them entirely.

It is not that I don't think people should follow their hearts— after all, our hearts are where Christ dwells when we invite Him to be Lord of our lives, and no decision should be made in life without consulting "our heart" on the matter. However, if we are honest, our hearts simply cannot be trusted as the final authority on many things—especially a marriage relationship. They simply are not reliable sources of information.

> Our hearts simply cannot be trusted as the final authority on many things—especially a marriage relationship.

Jeremiah 17:9 warns, "The heart is deceitful above all things and beyond cure. Who can understand it?" (NIV). Sometimes our hearts tell us to do something that does not mesh with what other (wiser) folks believe we should do. If we choose not to seek the counsel of others, and especially of the Holy Spirit, our hearts can lead us way off course in life. Why? Our hearts are usually in pursuit of one thing—*personal happiness*—both in life and in marriage.

We will talk more in question 31 about our relentless pursuit of happiness, but first notice how in the very next verse, God assures us, "I the LORD search the heart and examine the mind, to reward each person according to their conduct, according to what their deeds deserve" (Jeremiah 17:10 NIV). God is really the only One who can recognize what is truly operating in our hearts. He is the best emotional expert to help us discern *what* we are feeling, *why* we are feeling that way, and *how* to move forward with the best course of action.

If you have experienced the "What if my heart is telling me I married the wrong person?" question lately (and most humans admit entertaining this thought at various times in their marriage relationships), I encourage you to consider this: Your *heart* may be telling you to jump ship, but what is the *Lord* telling you to do?

The reason I ask is because of a precious principle I learned from a phenomenal book called *The Sacred Marriage* by Gary Thomas. He theorizes that marriage is not ultimately about our happiness—it is about our holiness.[1] It is about our willingness to let God use our presence in one another's lives to create a more Christlike character, to lovingly challenge each other, to purify our motives, to create more compassion in our lives, and to spur us on toward love and good deeds (Hebrews 10:24). A Spirit-led marriage simply transforms us both into the man and woman God ultimately wants us to become. There is no better refiner's fire than the institution of marriage. It turns immature boys and girls into fruitful men and women and transforms our self-centered natures into servants' hearts.

I know. I know. Being transformed is not always fun. It requires work. And energy. And patience. And humility. But do you know what *is* fun? Living a transformed life. Enjoying a transformed relationship. Resting in the security of a transformed marriage.

Revisiting Holly Holladay's blog once again, just listen to what fun she and Steve are having now that they have survived their transformation process:

> The moment was surreal. Conversation flowed freely and laughter filled the air as Steve and I shared an order of nachos. A last-minute date to a movie preview was followed by an impromptu late-night stop at a local taco stand. As we recounted the movie, we laughed so loud that other people began to stare. We were thoroughly enjoying each other's company! In that moment, I couldn't imagine being happier. I thought I might actually cry.

How did my marriage get from where it was to where it is? With a lot of hard work and determination! But now I can honestly say that, not only do I love my husband, I also like him and I respect him. We enjoy being together and don't need other people as a buffer. We have awesome conversations, we have a fantastic sex life, and we inspire each other to be better. We can argue without it threatening to ruin our relationship. And most importantly, we can just be. We can sit in silence without feeling the pain of a void. We don't have to worry about keeping up walls to protect ourselves. We have dreams and goals and without wishing time away, look forward to an empty nest.

When I think back to where we were compared to where we are, I feel like we deserve some kind of medal. There are moments when I want to stop and shout to everyone around, "Do you see how amazing this is?! Do you see how far my husband has come?" But really, it wasn't just him. It was both of us. We are reaping the fruits of labor from seeds that were sown in our tears. We made it. How? Because we didn't give up! More days than not, I thought it was over. The last time we went to counseling, my motivation was to justify divorce. Today reading that sentence brings tears to my eyes. If I had given up, I would have missed the absolute best years of my life. Yes, it was hard, but worth every minute. Every tear, every fit, every day that I thought I physically couldn't bear the pain anymore was worth it.

Things aren't perfect. But I know that there will be many more impromptu dates, moments of laughter, and cherished memories. No matter what life throws, I have faith in us. We will get through it. Together.[2]

I am so very proud of the progress Holly and Steve made in their marriage, along with hundreds of other couples I have had the privilege of coaching through their own unique marital crises.

Walter Bradford Cannon theorized that human nature's response to tension or stress is to "fight, freeze, or flee," also known as the "fight or flight" response.[3] Rather than running away or remaining stuck in a relational rut, I urge you to reconcile the issues troubling your marriage. Seek the help of a marital coach or counselor if necessary. Sure, there is usually some expense involved, but most couples (including Greg and me) will tell you that it has been the best money they have ever spent. In fact, if you think counseling is expensive, just wait until you see the price tag of divorce! *Whew!* Talk about an ounce of prevention being worth more than a pound of cure.

Earlier I posed a test question: "Your *heart* may be telling you to jump ship, but what is the *Lord* telling you to do?" Now I would like to end this section with a few more questions. Although some divorces are justifiable (such as in the case of unrepentant adultery or abuse), a greater percentage of divorcing couples simply run out of energy fighting for the relationship. They reach the end of their ropes. They decide to cash in their chips or gather up their toys and go home—alone. They would rather gamble on a more successful second attempt at marriage (or third or fourth) than ride out the storm until dawn bursts on the horizon. They just want to trade their current spouses in on a new-and-improved version and get on with a "happier" life.

But let me ask you this:

- What if you knew 100 percent that there would be no "next person in line"?

- What if this divorce really *is* the final chapter in your intimate relational experiences?
- If you were to take the Bible seriously about not having sex outside of marriage, and you were positive that this is where your sex life ends and your life of celibacy and singleness begins, would you still want to hit the eject button on this relationship?

Or

- Would you be willing to muster just a few more ounces of energy each day to iron out the wrinkles of your relationship? To make it work, for the benefit of both you and your spouse and for the glory of God?
- Would you like to grow up (mature) and grow old with your mate rather than spend your remaining years in loneliness and isolation?
- Wouldn't you prefer to hand a legacy of lasting marriage down to your children and grandchildren and great-grandchildren?

Take some time to meditate on those questions. Invite the Lord to "search your heart" as He promises He can. Open yourself wide to the possibilities. Imagine that marital bliss could be waiting just around the next counseling corner, just as Holly experienced.

As I was writing this in the Dallas/Fort Worth International Airport, I couldn't help but overhear a middle-aged single woman one row over declaring that so many of her married friends were always bemoaning how miserable they are with their current husbands. Eager to find a man with whom she can share her own life, she often responds (half in jest, half-serious), "If he's so horrible, honey, send him my way. I'll take him!" None of her friends had taken her up on the offer. But her point was well made. Many single people would give their right arms for the marital struggles that we have because, in their minds, even a remote chance at working through the challenging times and cultivating a rewarding marriage is better than no marriage at all.

So before you come to the final conclusion that Mr. or Mrs. Right is actually Mr. or Mrs. Wrong, consider what kind of long-term marital health benefits can result from some short-term marital strength conditioning. To help you envision what that might look like, and all that you could look forward to, keep reading.

31. WHAT IS THE SECRET TO STAYING TOGETHER FOREVER?

I was recently cohosting the morning show at the local radio station here in Tyler, Texas, with my dear friend Mike Harper, whom I frequently razz about how he "married *up*" when he found his wife, Lois. As usual I inquired about how she was doing. They had just received the joyful news that, after years of waiting, they were about to be grandparents, and Mike mentioned how much fun Lois was having "nesting" in preparation. He went on to make a comment that I will never forget, nor will I ever forget the look on his face when he said it. As if he was in absolute awe, he sweetly declared, "She is *so* good to me. I don't get it. I'll never get it. But she is *just so good* to me!"

Isn't that what we all hope our spouses would say about us, even when we are not around to receive the compliment? But this kind of love and passion for one another, spread out over decades of marriage, does not happen automatically. It requires intentionality, and without that intentionality, life takes a heavy toll on the relationship. We all have seen couples who have managed somehow to remain legally bound to one another, who dwell beneath the same roof, and who probably still sleep in the same bed. But when you watch them in a restaurant, they gaze over one another's shoulder in a daze, slightly agitated with the arrangement. They're together, but they're not. They're physically present, but mentally and emotionally they're oceans apart. They're spouses, but they aren't *friends*.

Making love is one thing. But making love *last* is the ultimate goal.

This obviously is not the type of relationship we longed for when we daydreamed of getting married and living happily ever after. Staying together is one thing. Staying interested is another. Making love is one thing. But making love *last* is the ultimate goal.

So how does a couple do that? As I have been contemplating that question, a few word pictures have come to mind. The first occurred one day as I was visiting my parents. As I coasted into their driveway, I noticed how the huge plot of land that they once relentlessly slaved over no longer bore any resemblance to the lush vegetable garden that it used to be. Each spring my dad tilled up the ground and fertilized the soil, and my mom carefully planted her onions, potatoes, tomatoes, and other vegetables that I failed to appreciate back then. Almost daily they watered the tender plants, hoed out the weeds, and picked bushel baskets full come harvesttime. We feasted all summer, sharing our bumper crops with the neighbors and canning the extras to last us through the winter.

Would it be realistic of me to think that I could go pluck a few cucumbers and ears of corn when that garden has not been touched in over a decade? No. The only thing that grows there now is grass. Once the labor ceased, the harvest did too. It does not take a rocket scientist to make the connection between my horticultural example and holy matrimony. We must be intentional about tending it . . . regularly. It is no secret that if you want your car to keep running, you must keep gas and oil in it, rather than letting it run dry. It is no secret that to keep a campfire burning, you need to stir the embers frequently, rather than leaving it unattended for long. Therefore, it should be no secret that to keep your relationship running smoothly and burning brightly, you must be intentional about fueling it regularly.

At this point some folks are hankering for a checklist. "Just tell me what to do, and I'll do it!" they declare. But such a checklist isn't the most effective prescription here. Each spouse's checklist would look different, based on his or her particular "love language." As author Gary Chapman explains in his book *The 5 Love Languages*, human beings have five primary ways of expressing affection toward one another:

- words of affirmation
- physical touch
- acts of service
- gifts
- quality time[4]

One person might say, "It means the most to me when you slow down and talk to me for a while." This person's love language is most likely *quality time* or *words of affirmation*. Another would say, "I don't enjoy talking that much, but I like it when you do things for me, especially when you give me a back rub or initiate sex." This person obviously prefers *acts of service* and *physical touch*. What we need to remember is to speak the *other* person's love language, not just our own, in order for it to be truly perceived as the loving gesture we intend. This is true not just with our spouses but with our children and friends as well.

So if you are the type of person who needs a checklist, get your spouse to create one for you. Ask, "What are ten things that I could do that would make you feel incredibly loved?" Then keep that list handy and refer back to it often until speaking your spouse's love language comes almost as naturally as speaking your own.

But an even more effective approach than checking things off of a cheat sheet is the kind of attitude you hold toward your spouse. Let's face it . . . if you are a crab or a jerk to your mate on a recurring basis, no act of service or tangible gift glosses over that dynamic. As the Bible tells us:

A quarreling wife [or husband] is as bothersome
as a continual dripping on a rainy day. (Proverbs 27:15 NCV)

It is better to live alone in the desert than with a quarreling
and complaining wife [or husband]. (Proverbs 21:19 NCV)

If you want to make sure you are not poking holes in your own bucket of marital bliss, discern which of the three attitudes describes you—stingy, fair, or generous:

1. Stingy Spouses are those who, quite frankly, feel as if the world revolves around them. Their mates exist mainly for the purpose of meeting their needs, and they get upset when this isn't being properly demonstrated on a regular basis. They might sound something like this:

   • "Where's dinner? Where's my clean laundry?"
   • "Why is the house such a wreck? What have you been doing all day?"
   • "Why don't you make more money?"
   • "Why don't you help me with the kids more?"
   • "Why aren't you willing to have sex with me more often?"
   • "Can you not see that I need you to _____?" (Fill in the blank)

2. Fair Spouses are a huge improvement over Stingy Spouses. Fair Spouses are happy to shoulder their share of the marital/parenting/domestic load. But they have an ulterior motive. They subconsciously keep score to make sure everything stays Even/Steven between them. So they dole out attention and affection only in direct proportion to how much they feel their partners deserve it on any given day. These husbands or wives may sound something like this:

   • "I took care of that yesterday, so why aren't you taking the initiative to do it today? It's your turn."
   • "I'm the one who makes most of the money, so why shouldn't I get to decide how we spend it?"

- "If you would help more around the house, I wouldn't be too tired to have sex."
- "How can you expect me to _____ when you won't _____?"

3. Generous Spouses are those who exemplify a desire to serve, rather than seeking to be served. It is never about keeping score to make sure things are fair. Rather, it is about earning brownie points by seeing how often and in how many ways they can delight their mates. They are very effective at *inspiring* cooperation rather than *requiring* it, which is a far more effective approach. Here are some examples of what Generous Spouses might sound like:

- "Is there anything I can do for you to make life a little easier right now?"
- "You've been working hard lately. Why don't you take a few hours this weekend to recharge your batteries?"
- "I've been having all kinds of racy thoughts about what I'd like to do to you tonight!"
- "All my emotional eggs are in your basket, babe. You're *it* for me!"

Sometimes we can exhibit all three of these attitudes in the same day, but what would it look like if our main goal in marriage was to strive toward being that Generous Spouse as often as possible? What if pressing the pause button to give thoughtful consideration toward some way to bless our mates became a natural part of our days, just like brushing our teeth or making breakfast or feeding the cat? I think that through such simple endeavors, we would discover that the real secret to staying together forever is simply to have a wild, passionate love affair . . . with our spouses . . . every single day.

Being a "words of affirmation" girl, I enjoyed reading one of the sweetest little love stories in a devotional book that Greg and I read together long ago, called *Night Light: A Devotional for Couples* by Dr. James Dobson. Narrated by the granddaughter of an elderly couple, the story explains the competition that went on in her grandparents' house over many years. Upon visiting, she recalled finding the letters "S.H.M.I.L.Y." in random places—written in the fogged-up bathroom mirror, traced in the surface of the flour canister, and elsewhere. It wasn't until years later that she finally learned what this secret code meant between her grandmother and grandfather. S.H.M.I.L.Y. stood for "See How Much I Love You?" They were intentional about generously sharing this sentiment with one another, and because they eagerly managed the garden of their love, they were able to feast off of the abundant harvest for decades.[5]

With "gifts" also ranking high on my list of native love languages, Greg scored some major brownie points recently with an unexpected surprise. The night before, I had bemoaned the fact that every time I tried to cook a steak on my George Foreman grill, it came out incredibly tough, no matter what kind of seasoning or marinade I used. I was about ready to retire from my steak-cooking days and just stick with chicken or fish. But lo and behold, I discovered a new gadget on the kitchen counter the very next day. It had a long, white handle on top, with lots of spikes on the bottom, and I immediately recognized it as a meat tenderizer. I melted. Amazing how a tiny investment of $11.99 can reap such relational interest.

Greg's love language is acts of service, so I win his heart when I detail his car, take his shirts to the dry cleaner, or deliver dinner to his office on the nights he winds up having to work late. When you know your spouse's love language, figuring out just how to say, "I love you" isn't a mystery. It is amazing how that tidbit of knowledge, a little consideration, and the execution of a simple little plan communicate volumes to your spouse.

Whether it is speaking the other person's love language, paying attention to your mate's needs and desires and eagerly fulfilling them, or being a generous, adventurous, and fulfilling sex partner—there is simply no *one* particular way to be a perfect spouse—but there are a million ways to be a darn good one.

PONDER THE PRINCIPLE

- What are some of the things your spouse has done in the past that have made you feel incredibly loved, cherished, or celebrated?
- What are some things you would love your spouse to do in the future to create similar feelings of joy and relational security?
- What is something that you particularly enjoy doing for your spouse simply because it makes you feel good about investing in the relationship?

PASSION PRINCIPLE #4:

Celebrate the Physical Side of Sex

Hygiene 101

32. HOW CAN I BRING MY *A-GAME* INTO THE BEDROOM?

STUCK IN INFAMOUS LOS ANGELES TRAFFIC, IT SEEMED LISTENING to a sex therapy radio talk show was the only productive way to pass the time. A woman called in complaining that her husband rarely performs oral sex (more about oral sex is yet to come), but frequently desires her to perform it for him. She couldn't understand how things had gotten so one-sided in their marriage bed, and she was demanding change (and prepared to hold out on him until that change took place).

The therapist asked in response, "Could there be a feminine hygiene issue?"

The caller was dead silent. Finally she asked, "What do you mean?"

The therapist responded, "Do you cleanse your vaginal area properly before expecting your husband to perform oral sex?"

Again, dead silence.

She eventually replied, "Well, I take a shower, if that's what you mean."

"No, I'm not talking about just a shower. Do you spread the

lips of your vagina and use some sort of body wash to get rid of the odor and bacteria naturally present there?" the therapist inquired, leaving no room for misinterpretation.

The caller replied, "I was never told that was necessary, and I heard Dr. Oz say on *Oprah* that the vagina is a 'self-cleaning oven.'"

I thought, *Hello? This woman is expecting her husband to indulge in such an intimate sexual act with his mouth (and nose) when she hasn't properly cleansed herself?* In all honesty, I wanted to find this gal's mama, spank her, and ask, "What were you thinking to let your daughter wander into marriage without even a basic understanding of feminine hygiene?"

And then I thought, *Oh, her poor husband!* I wanted to scream four simple words loud enough so that she could hear me in Philadelphia all the way from Los Angeles: "Summer's Eve intimate cleanser!"

In case this is a news flash for you, let me explain a few things:

- Yes, the vaginal *canal* is a self-cleaning oven, but the "oven door" has to be wiped down regularly. The vaginal lips (the internal and external folds of skin surrounding the vaginal canal) collect sweat and bacteria like any other crack or crevice of your body. Not to get too gross here, but you would not expect your husband to lick between your toes or under your armpits unless they had been thoroughly washed with soap and water, right? A wife should have standards just as sensitive with her nether region.

- Doctors recommend that women should not douche more than once a month (if at all) because inserting those chemicals inside your vaginal canal washes away all your natural (good) bacteria that fight off infections. What I am talking about here isn't using an internal douche. It is simply cleansing in between the folds of skin to eliminate foul odors (and tastes).

- If you desire oral sex from your husband (not all women do, and that is okay), also realize that in addition to proper cleansing, keeping your pubic hair neatly coiffed would probably make the experience far more pleasurable for him. I cannot imagine anyone enjoying a mouthful of pubic hair, so if you are going to feed him a picnic on the lawn, trim the grass!

This leads us to another woman's e-mail:

I have some questions concerning body hair. I have been told to shave or wax down there. I have shaved it a few times, but it just leaves a rash and itches like crazy when it comes back. So I'm not sure how to keep myself groomed in that area. Is there a certain kind of tool to use in order to keep yourself groomed or would you suggest maybe Nair? This is rather awkward for me to ask, but I figure other wives want to know as well!

This is a great question. So here is my opinion on several different options:

- Hair-removing lotion: These products are only meant for external hair, such as legs or armpits. I wouldn't go there with the vaginal area—too much possibility for a negative reaction to such harsh chemicals.
- Shaving: Not only is it difficult to shave yourself, but you're right—it feels great for a few hours; then the rash sets in,

and you are stuck with three days of major crotch-itch until it grows back. Miserable!

- Waxing: Yes, I tried it. Once. And I can't say I will ever do it again. I was *so* eager to hear my cosmetologist say those three magical words: "We're all done!" Even though waxing feels great afterward and lasts a good while, in my opinion, the process ranks right up there with root canals, Chinese water torture, and bamboo shoots under your fingernails. If you have a low tolerance for pain, waxing may not be for you.

So what is a gal to do if none of these are great options? Try these quick-trim techniques:

- After showering and using an intimate cleansing product like Summer's Eve intimate cleanser, grab sections of pubic hair between two fingers and gently pull them away from the body. Then use regular haircutting scissors to trim as close to your skin as possible without cutting yourself. It will create a "low-burr haircut" effect.
- Stand over the toilet so that hair falls directly into the bowl to make cleanup a snap.
- You could also use a man's beard trimmer for such a job, but do *not* stand over a small body of water, such as a toilet, to use an electrical appliance.
- Slip back into the shower for another quick cleansing session to wash away any remaining stray stubble.

No harsh chemicals, no painful waxing, no razor burn, no horrible itch as it grows out! Every two to four weeks should be plenty to keep your private playground well groomed. You might also try the new Schick Quatro razor, which I understand is a battery-powered trimmer that is waterproof, so you can use it in the shower.

If reaching these parts of your body is a challenge for you, hand your husband the scissors with a smile, place a towel on the bed, lie down on your back, and invite him to give you a hand. Most men would be happy to oblige, knowing they will get to indulge afterward.

REAL MEN EXERCISE PROPER HYGIENE TOO

Sexual hygiene is not just a woman's concern. Husbands need to be aware of what they can do to make sexual intimacy a more appealing and pleasurable experience for their partners as well. As one (anonymous) woman wrote:

> It's really disgusting when we're in the heat of passion, and I discover his need for a shower! I mean, come on! Do men think that skid-marked underwear and dingleberries are a turn-on? I don't want to embarrass him, but I'm realizing lately that if my husband wants me to take a nosedive, he's going to have to make it more tolerable for my nose!

Husbands, please, don't be *that guy*! Your wife should feel that she married a full-grown man, not a big toddler who needs a diaper change. So here are some pointers for you:

- If you are hoping for sex before going to sleep at night (or upon waking up in the morning), take a shower before getting into bed. It will increase your chances greatly if you don't reek of any kind of sweat (or worse).

- Just as we advised the ladies, use soap or some sort of cleanser in every crack or crevice that you are hoping your wife will come into close contact with. Dry toilet paper simply is not enough to truly cleanse a big, hairy bottom.
- It will also help for you to keep the hair around your anus well trimmed so you can avoid "dingleberry formation" altogether. Consider buying a separate razor especially for this purpose.
- Keeping the pubic hair around the base of your penis and scrotum under control (known as "manscaping") will be the sexual equivalent of rolling out the red carpet for your wife.

There you have it, ladies and gentlemen! This might have been far more than you ever really wanted to know about sexual hygiene, and most likely far more than your mama ever thought to tell you. But I would be willing to bet that your spouse will be so glad that *someone* told you so that you can both enjoy some good, clean fun as you indulge in these passion principles.

33. HOW CAN WE ENJOY THE *AFTERGLOW* WITHOUT THE *AFTER-MESS*?

It is always interesting to hear from newlyweds *after* the honeymoon. Most brides and grooms wander into marriage assuming that their whirlwind sexual encounters will be identical to what they have witnessed in the movies. Everything fits together perfectly, they soon climax simultaneously, and then they get to lie blissfully on the bed together in each other's arms until they drift off to sleep with big smiles on their faces.

But this e-mail I received from one wife illustrates that things rarely play out so neatly:

> I'm a newlywed, and I am quite surprised by what a mess sex creates! I always feel like I have to get right up and go to the bathroom to clean off within minutes of having sex, or else our sheets are going to get all messed up, and I'd have to do laundry practically every other day! And I can't go to sleep without being dry and clean down there, so what's a girl to do?

Yeah, I don't know of many spouses who *don't* share this same sentiment, at least to a certain degree. So here are a few suggestions to take care of the after-mess quickly and completely so you can get back to enjoying the afterglow together:

- When it comes to bedtime sex, husbands, consider "making your deposit" externally rather than internally. Ejaculating onto your wife's abdomen will make cleanup much easier, and then she isn't awakened in the middle of the night by . . . well, you know.
- In your nightstand drawer keep a short stack of old washcloths or dish towels. When the climaxes are over, quick cleanup is a breeze, and these cloths can just be tossed into the hamper and laundered each week with the rest of the towels.
- Remember that baby wipes are not just for babies. If you prefer a moist cleanup over a dry one, keep a container of baby wipes nearby. (These are also handy for when you want to indulge in some intimate moments before showers have taken place, so these can be useful both before and after sex.)

- Speaking of baby stuff, also keep a few waterproof crib pads underneath your bed. It is the perfect sheet protector to tuck under your bottom beforehand and is much more effective than just a terry-cloth towel at making sure neither of you is stuck sleeping in the wet spot all night.

Since originally posting some of these ideas on my blog, a few follow-up suggestions came from readers:

- "For major neatniks, forget the tissues, which disintegrate too easily, and keep a roll of paper towels under your bed instead. Tear off a sheet or two prior to getting the party started, and tuck it under your pillow or wherever you can get to it quickly as needed. When things heat up, place the paper towel either on his tummy or on hers (based on which sexual position you are in as you are about to cross the finish line), and then when the geyser erupts, the fluid goes directly onto the paper towel, preventing the personal mess from getting very messy at all. This is especially helpful for the guy with the hairy belly who doesn't want to feel crusty all night."
- "When my wife got her tubes tied, I was pretty excited not to have to use condoms any longer. However, when I realized what a great job they did keeping the semen completely contained, I went back to using them for this purpose rather than for birth control. Pinching the tip, slipping it off, and tossing it afterward just seems so much easier than trying to mop up the mess."
- "When my husband asked why I wasn't as sexually

interested as I used to be, I paused to do a quick soul-search and realized it was because I'd gotten really lazy—not about having sex, but about cleaning up after sex. It just seemed such a bother to strip the wet sheets off, find clean ones, put them all in place, and so forth. So one day I came up with a brilliant idea! Whenever I go out for a walk in the cold, I dress in at least two or three layers so I can start shucking one layer at a time as I warm up and begin to sweat a little. So why couldn't I do the same with our master bed? I purchased an extra set of sheets and a waterproof mattress protector, then layered the bed like a linen lasagna—one fitted sheet, followed by the mattress protector, then another fitted sheet. So now if things get a little damp, all I have to do is strip off the top two layers, toss them in the dirty laundry hamper, and crawl back into bed! I still have fresh sheets to sleep on without having to go rummaging through linen closets or wrestling sheet pockets over mattress corners (which isn't my idea of a relaxing bedtime activity)."

Some of these ideas may sound a little extreme, but necessity *is* the mother of invention. Just as an artist keeps his drop cloths and mineral spirits near his easel or as a chef keeps his countertops wiped down as he is working along, a smart couple keeps certain tools handy to ensure passion and productivity. Keeping things nice, neat, clean, and comfortable is key to creating the perfect lovemaking environment, so kudos to those who are willing to think outside the box in order to avoid stressing over the mess.

PONDER THE PRINCIPLE

◆ Is there any hygiene issue that you have wanted to discuss with your spouse but were afraid of bringing it up? If so, do the past two sections give you the courage to speak what is on your mind?

◆ What are some of the things your spouse does to keep things neat and clean in the marriage bed that you really appreciate?

◆ What hygiene ideas stood out to you as something you would like to incorporate into your lovemaking repertoire?

Eureka!

34. HOW CAN I (RE)DISCOVER MY SPOUSE'S SEXUAL HOT SPOTS?

I HEAR MANY COUPLES BEMOANING THE FACT THAT THINGS JUST aren't as "hot" between them since they got married. They reminisce about their season of dating and how the urge to have sex with each other felt absolutely, positively overwhelming at times. Yet after the vows were exchanged, the sexual tension disappeared. They wonder, "Where has the spark gone? And can we ignite it once again?"

We first have to accept the fact that marital relationships naturally go through peaks and valleys, ups and downs, and sexual highs and lows. But when we experience those sexual lows, we do not have to stay there. We *can* return to a season of marital and sexual bliss.

We know because we recently did just that—accidentally.

When I had a hysterectomy in 2012, my doctor warned me, "No sexual activity for a minimum of six weeks." So I braced myself for a l-o-n-g dry spell. But what we soon noticed was that because we knew we couldn't have intercourse, we focused a lot more attention on all the other things we could do without crossing that line.

We kissed. A lot. Long, sweet, slow kisses. And it really got our juices flowing. Kind of like when we were dating and would find ourselves *so* aroused by one another. And we caressed and touched a lot more. We weren't in a mad rush to hurry up and go straight to intercourse because we knew we couldn't. And this got our juices flowing all the more.

> Marital relationships naturally go through peaks and valleys, ups and downs, and sexual highs and lows. But when we experience those sexual lows, we do not have to stay there.

And we talked. A lot more than before. Mostly about how great it was going to be when we could have sex again. But I did not want to go back to sex as usual. I wanted us to take these valuable lessons into this next season. Great sex is not just about the penis going inside the vagina. It is about the wet, wonderful kisses . . . the soft, gentle caresses . . . the sweet, intimate words exchanged . . . the passion that is stirred when two people take their time to really discover—or rediscover—how to get each other's sexual motor revving high.

So to find that sexual *high gear* once again, perhaps you should kick things down into *low* gear for a while—at least until your sexual motor has a chance to really get revving once again. S-l-o-w down, and rediscover the *fun* of foreplay.

I asked several women and men to share their favorite foreplay activity, and here are a few responses:

- "I love it when my husband holds my hand or puts his arm around me when we're sitting on the couch watching TV. It makes me feel like I did when we were courting."

- "When my wife kisses me and the 'peck' kiss turns into a 'French' kiss, I go weak in the knees! When she initiates that kind of kiss, I pretty much know that I'm not going to be turned down for sex, and that gives me confidence to go for it!"

- "When I'm doing dishes at the kitchen sink, I love it when my husband wraps his arms around me from behind and kisses the back of my neck."

- "There's something about being touched along the sides of my body from underneath my arms down the sides of my rib cage down to my hips and thighs—that drives me wild. There's no way my husband can touch me like that and not send shivers down my spine."

- "Ironically, we both have the same sexual hot spot. We both love for our nipples to be caressed with either the fingers or the tongue. We've even figured out how to position ourselves so we both can do that for one another, simultaneously!"

- "I love it when my wife lets her hair down and brushes out all of the sticky stuff so I can just play with it between my fingers. To me, touching her hair is almost as sexy as touching her more intimate body parts."

- "I am transported to another place and time when my husband approaches me, gently laces his fingers around my neck and jawline, brushes my cheek with his thumbs, and plants a sweet kiss on the tip of my nose."

Yeah, everyone has his or her particular "hot spots" or a movement that turns the most mundane of evenings into something magical. For me, it is a long, strong foot rub with big, masculine hands, especially when Greg gently rubs lotion in between each one of my toes. For him, it is when I caress his earlobe with my lips or gently massage his hairy chest.

Eventually enough hot spots are discovered and sexual steam builds up that moving to more intimate hot spots simply can't be helped. When that happens, there are three points in particular on a woman's body that her man should know about, and three spots on a man's body that his woman should be well aware of.

Before I spell them out for you, I had to laugh at an e-mail I received recently. Eager to be a good "student" of her husband's body, a woman handed her husband a tube of lipstick on their anniversary. She sent him into the bathroom, saying, "Draw me a map of where you want me to touch you most." He disappeared, then exuberantly emerged sixty seconds later with a big smile on his face and hot-pink lipstick on every square inch of his genital area.

Many men report that *any* part of the penis being touched is pleasurable, but most will say that these are the top three favorites:

- The frenulum. This is the place with the highest density of nerve endings on a man's body. The frenulum is found on the underside of the penis, just behind the head. Experts suggest that you approach this area with caution, as many men report that it is so sensitive that they don't enjoy too much direct stimulation, but rather a gentler touch.[1]
- The head. When babies are conceived, both males and females are identical. Their genitalia are exactly the same until the ninth week of gestation, when chromosomal differences cause what is the "clitoris" on the female

(explained in the next section) to "sprout" and become a male penis.[2] Therefore, the uppermost inch or so of the tip of the penis (called the "head") is the most sexually sensitive, especially around the rim of the circumcised penis.

• The "seam." This hot spot is found on the underside of the scrotum (the skin that contains his testicles or "balls") in the small section of his body between the testicles and the anus. If you look carefully, you will see a significant line running along that area, which almost appears to be a seam, where God stitched men up! If a couple can position themselves to allow it, slightly stroking this section adds significantly to his sexual pleasure.

The best way to determine your husband's hottest hot spots is to do just as the woman I mentioned earlier did. Simply *ask him* to show you. Hopefully he won't use up all your best lipstick providing an answer to that question.

A woman's body can seem a bit more mysterious when it comes to her hot spots, but once these places are identified, they are really not that difficult to find or stimulate. Her primary points of pleasure are:

• The clitoris. About the size of an eraser on the tip of a pencil, the clitoris is merely a collection of nerves that creates a tiny pink bump just inside the labia (the folds of skin on the exterior vaginal area). The best way to discover it is simply for a woman to explore this region with her fingers in the presence of her partner, and then point out the tiny section that is most sensitive to the touch. What purpose does the clitoris serve? Interestingly enough, it exists for absolutely *no* biological reason other than to provide women great pleasure through clitoral stimulation and resulting orgasm.[3] Most women report that because this is such a highly sensitive area, they prefer a variety of movements (back and forth, side to side, and circular motions) to stimulate this hot spot rather than merely an elevator-button-pushing approach.

- The G-spot. While still a mystery to many married couples, the G-spot really does exist. It is not just something that a German gynecologist by the name of Ernst Gräfenberg made up. It is an erogenous zone located approximately one to three inches inside the anterior wall of the vaginal canal (toward her belly button). When stimulated for long enough (done most effectively with the pad of the middle finger in a "hook" position so that it is putting slight pressure on that anterior wall), it can result in a vaginal orgasm and expulsion of a significant amount of fluid (referred to as "female ejaculation"). Be sure to have towels or a waterproof pad handy. Unlike the clitoris, the G-spot is more easily discovered by the husband's finger than by the wife's own finger.

- The perineum. Just as the section between a man's penis and anus are sexually sensitive due to the vast number of nerve endings present, the tiny section between a woman's vaginal canal and anus is usually considered a hot spot as well.

With some intentionality and imagination, both the G-spot and the clitoris can be stimulated such that a woman experiences both a G-spot orgasm and a clitoral orgasm simultaneously, sometimes referred to as a "blended orgasm" or "double orgasm."

For more information about male anatomy, female anatomy,

and especially how a woman can experience orgasm, check out the chapter titled "Experiencing the Big 'Oh!'" in my book *The Sexually Confident Wife*.[4]

Of course, every person is different when it comes to hot spots—where and how he or she likes to be touched. The way to discover what floats your spouse's sexual boat the most isn't to read a book or manual or even surf the Internet. The absolute best, most surefire way to zero in on that magical spot or movement is to simply ask your spouse since his or her opinion is really the only one that counts. Consider the following statements together and take turns filling in the blanks:

> The absolute best, most surefire way to zero in on that magical spot or movement is to simply ask your spouse.

- When you touch me here (_____), it drives me wild.
- When you do this (_____), I can't help but get turned on.
- I love it when you let me _____. It makes me feel _____.

Another idea is to take your spouse's hand in yours and give him or her a guided tour of your own body, focusing on the spots that crave the most attention. Or simply give your spouse a peep show of what you like best, performing it on yourself for his or her visual entertainment.

Now, if that last part made you blush, let me give a quick disclaimer here. I know some couples have a lot of hang-ups about masturbation and choose not to engage in it at all, and I completely understand if that is how you feel. But what I am encouraging you to do is not to separate yourself from your spouse and self-ishly take matters into your own hands. There is a big difference between solo masturbation and self-stimulation in the presence of your spouse. In fact, most couples report that watching their spouses turn themselves on is quite the erotic experience.

The bottom line is that we simply need to slow down and carve out some special time together—in bed, on the couch, in the bathtub or shower, on a weekend getaway—for the sole purpose of the sexual exploration of each other's bodies. Think of yourself as Christopher Columbus, charting new territory and making note of every interesting discovery you come upon.

35. HOW CAN WE BALANCE MISMATCHED SEX DRIVES?

Remembering that each person's sexuality is as unique as a finger-print, let's consider for a moment the wide variety of complexities involved in a person's sexuality. First there is the family we grew up in and what our parents taught us (or failed to teach us) about sex. Then there is what our siblings and peers taught us, as well as whatever our pastors, Sunday school teachers, youth group leaders, or other spiritual or moral influences may have taught us. And, of course, we cannot leave out the sexual messages we were exposed to through a wide variety of media outlets.

We also must take into consideration the gender-specific messages we received from the culture we grew up in. Now toss in the fact that you are a certain age and in a certain season of marriage. Some of us are "dinks" (double income, no kids), others are in the thick of parenting, and still others are empty nesters.

Obviously there are a *lot* of factors playing into just how sexual we may feel during certain times of our lives. And the thing is—it is *always* changing. How we feel sexually in our twenties is not the same as how we feel in our thirties, forties, fifties, sixties—and beyond for many folks, God bless them!

With that being said, hopefully you understand why I think sexual stereotypes are incredibly unfair. As mentioned previously, what sexual stereotype is most common? All men want sex. All women do not. Husbands are sexually frustrated. Wives couldn't care less. Isn't that the message presented on most TV sitcoms and in movie theaters? In my coaching practice, however, I would say there is about a 50/50 split. Granted, some couples complain that *he* wants sex far more often than *she* does. But at least half of my coaching clients say *she* is the one wanting sex more often, and the husband is the one with the lower libido.

Notice I did not title this section, "What if one of us wants sex more than the other?" That can be the case from one day to the next. Sometimes he is feeling frisky and she is feeling frigid that night, and the next day it easily can be vice versa. These differences can be ironed out as we practice mutual submission in a sexual sense. It is a lot healthier for a spouse to simply muster the energy to cooperate for the benefit of his or her spouse's sexual release than for "not tonight" to become so standard of a response that sexual tension builds to the point of resentment in the relationship.

Instead, I chose to phrase the question: "How can we balance mismatched sex drives?" This terminology indicates that it is not just an occasional "one wants it; the other doesn't" kind of issue. It is more like a "we simply aren't on the same page sexually during this season of our lives, and it has become a burr underneath our marital saddle." So let's examine what could be going on, and what can be done to improve the situation.

WHEN *SHE* WANTS MORE

There are many reasons why a man may be struggling with low libido in the marriage bed, particularly:

- the use of pornography
- excessive masturbation
- depression
- anxiety about work
- health issues
- weight issues

Any of these can create a hole in a man's sexual bucket, draining him of most of the sexual energy that his wife longs for. Remedying these issues can be rather complex, but it can also be relatively obvious. If he is exerting most of his sexual energy looking at other women and taking matters into his own hands through pornography and masturbation, he needs to disconnect from those isolating behaviors and learn to reconnect with the real, live woman to whom he is married. If depression or anxiety is what is draining him, a counselor can provide a couple with practical tools to cope with those emotional roller-coaster rides. If health or weight issues are the main challenges, a doctor or nutritionist may provide the keys to a healthier lifestyle, and such changes usually naturally result in rejuvenated sexual interest.

However, there is one main issue that often robs a man of his sexual desire that no one else on the planet can cure (other than the woman he is married to). When a man feels sexually insecure or emotionally disconnected from his wife, it can certainly wreak havoc on the marriage bed. Here are a couple of testimonies I gathered while writing *Every Woman's Marriage* that illustrate my point:

- Bill writes: "In my relationship with my wife, Lydia, our 'dance' more often feels to me like she is more interested in control than oneness, which feels devastating. I feel as if I am her puppet on a string. . . . How do I continue pursuing oneness with her when oneness with me isn't in her agenda?

  "The second area is very confusing to me. Lydia actually has a greater appetite for sex than I do. While we have had some wonderful lovemaking, there have been many times where my lack of performance or foreplay technique has enraged Lydia. On more than one occasion she has derided me for having a short penis. All of this makes the whole idea of having sex with my wife a risky proposition that just as often deflates my confidence as boosts it and makes me feel humiliated and emasculated. In the past she has demanded that I read books about foreplay and sex (which I have) and initiate sex more . . . be sexier by what I wear, how I sit, and how I talk or walk.

  "A doctor discovered that my testosterone level is very low for my age (we don't know why—stress?). I started taking testosterone to bring it back up. While that has had the effect of elevating the need for release, it has had a limited effect on increasing my sexual desire for Lydia. We have not had sex in a few months. She's even threatened to go have sex with someone else if I don't perform better and more frequently. I've tried to relate to her the impact all this has had on me and on my motivation to pursue her sexually, but she shifts the blame and refuses to see her part in all of this."

- Ray's words also confirm that there are often emotional issues that dampen a husband's sexual passion. He e-mails:

"Sure, I want a passionate sexual connection with my wife just as badly as the next guy, but it takes more than a little physical stimulation to make up for the hurt that she causes me before we ever go to bed at night. My wife's 'constructive criticism' is usually anything but constructive. Her expectations are so unrealistic that no man could ever live up to her standards. She uses the Bible as a weapon against what she perceives as my shortcomings. When I offer to pray with her, she feels the need to pray out loud (obviously both to God and to me) for my many weaknesses.

"Women assume that our hearts and penises are made of steel and completely disconnected from one another, but they are not. It can be just as difficult for a man to get aroused by the woman who makes his heart grow cold as it is for a woman to open herself sexually when she feels no intimate connection with her husband. There's been a lot of emphasis on how men and women are different, but we're really not that different when it comes to needing to feel somewhat appreciated and affirmed in order to feel sexually aroused."[5]

Ray is right. There is much more to pleasing our husbands than just being willing to engage in intercourse. Physical pleasure should be the dessert enjoyed after the appetizer of appreciation, the entrée of encouragement and unconditional love, and the side dish of respect. Any man who is starved of the other courses of the meal and given only dessert will eventually become an undernourished husband.

A man's lack of interest also simply may be due to the fact that he is aging, and part of the aging process means that he does not produce as much testosterone, the hormone mainly responsible for our sex drives. The problem is that a woman may be approaching her sexual peak (often in her forties or fifties) just as a man is slowing down. It can seem quite unfair.

So my gentle reminder to men is, even if you feel your sex drive slowing down, pay attention to what your wife's sex drive may be doing. Even if you lose your ability to maintain a penile erection, that doesn't mean that all the fun has to come to a screeching halt. Your wife still has sexual needs and desires. And you still have perfect use of your fingers, your hands, your lips, your tongue. Most wives can sympathize with a natural decline in erectile functioning as their husbands age. What they don't understand is how their husbands can choose to ignore or reject them sexually, insisting on bench warming when they are still very much interested in playing the game.

WHEN *HE* WANTS MORE

There is also a wide variety of issues that could be draining a woman of her sexual energy, which ironically are not that different from the list for men—pornography and masturbation, depression, stress, and other emotional roller-coaster rides due to work or family, or health and weight issues that rob her of physical energy. And the remedies for these issues are not very different either. Sometimes we simply need to recruit the help of a trained professional to overcome the hurdles holding us back in the bedroom.

But I find that there is a common myth that women have come to believe about female sexuality, and I believe it is the number-one thing holding most women back when their husbands want to be sexually intimate more often. What is that myth? I can name that tune in three words: "Good girls don't!"

Isn't that what we are told . . . over and over and over? By parents who truly loved us but were more concerned about our getting pregnant and tarnishing the family name than raising us up to be sexually healthy wives. I still cringe when I remember my mom chanting, "He won't buy the cow if you give him the milk for free!" (Which, granted, can be true, but I never liked being compared to livestock.) My dad would also jokingly call out from the porch as I was leaving on dates, "Keep your legs crossed and your panties on, now, you hear?" What I actually heard was, "Be a good girl! Don't have sex!"

If you received a similar message growing up, perhaps you are like me. I rebelled as a single gal, trying to prove that good girls *do* have sex. But then I got married, and I didn't want my husband to think I was a "bad girl," so my sexual pendulum swung in the opposite direction. My lifestyle fully supported the notion that Satan's favorite strategy is this: *Make single women think they can't live without sex. Make married women think they can.*

But sexuality is not Satan's domain. He borrowed it from God and has been distorting it since the book of Genesis. According to God's sexual economy, single women *can* live without sex, and married women *can* enjoy it—*freely!* No guilt, no shame, no inhibition. So rather than "Good girls don't!" rolling around in my subconscious, my new mantra has become: *Good (married) girls do have sex! They do it often, and they do it well, and they enjoy it!*

A similar myth is that "sex is just something women should do for their husbands. We don't really get anything out of it." That is why it feels like a chore to most wives. I have had some women tell me that if they had to choose between sex and sweeping the floors, bathing children, or folding laundry, they would pick housework over their husbands.

If you fall into this category, may I please give you a news flash? Women get a *lot* out of sex! Or at least they should. In addition to the mental, emotional, and spiritual health benefits women derive from marital intimacy, it can even be argued that women get just as much physically—perhaps even *more*—out of sex as men do.

Although Sigmund Freud accused women of having "penis envy," I completely disagree that a guy's body is designed to experience more sexual pleasure than women. Why? Consider these facts:

- Women are capable of experiencing one sexual climax after another (referred to as "multiple orgasms") until she has decided she has had enough, whereas men must sit things out sexually to recuperate before experiencing another round of pleasure (referred to as a "refractory period").[6]
- Women have *two* ways to experience orgasm (clitoral and G-spot orgasms), whereas men only have one basic way.[7]
- The clitoris is estimated to contain approximately eight thousand nerve fibers, which is more than *twice* as many nerves as are in a man's penis.[8]

Yeah, God loves us that much, ladies, and He intends for us to enjoy sex every bit as much as our husbands. Perhaps maybe even *twice* as much, huh? So I am not buying the "penis envy" concept. Natalie Angier, author of the book *Women: An Intimate Geography*, obviously shares my sentiment. In response to the notion of penis envy, she says, "Who would want a shotgun when you can have a semiautomatic?"[9]

I also have some words of wisdom for husbands on this topic. The reason most women feel "put upon" sexually (rather than being totally in touch with all of these sexy hot spots we have been talking about) is because some men are rather selfish when it comes to sex. It's all about them and their pleasure, rather than taking the time to study and pleasure their partners. Over the past twenty years many women have confessed to me that their husbands' idea of foreplay is to pout and beg, "Just lie there for five minutes and let me do what I need to do. That's all I'm asking!" Not sexy. *So* not sexy. No woman wants to feel like a sexual doormat.

In addition to the mental, emotional, and spiritual health benefits women derive from marital intimacy, it can even be argued that women get just as much physically—perhaps even *more*—out of sex as men do.

According to Jewish tradition, sexual satisfaction is actually the *woman's* right in a marriage. If you want your wife to be an interested and motivated sex partner, simply make sure that *she* is enjoying the sexual experience every bit as much as you. Then pouting or begging will *never* have to be part of your sexual repertoire.

Dear Lord, please show us how to truly minister to one another sexually, paying more attention to the other's needs than to our own. When our sexual desires are aroused, show us how to inspire rather than require the intimacy that we long for. When our sexual desires plummet, give us the grace to communicate exactly what we are in need of to feel reconnected and reenergized. And as our physical interest waxes and wanes from one season to the next, keep our hearts and spirits fully connected to one another for Your glory. Amen.

36. WILL HAVING CHILDREN NEGATIVELY AFFECT OUR SEX LIFE?

With the buzz it generated on everything from morning news programs to late-night talk shows, I am guessing it will go down as one of the most memorable moments in TV sitcom history. It was the fall 2011 season of ABC's *Modern Family*, and the Dunphy children—teens Haley and Alex and preadolescent Luke—were about to surprise their parents with a breakfast-in-bed tray to celebrate their wedding anniversary. As they gingerly opened the bedroom door, however, the big surprise wasn't the kind act of service they were bestowing upon their parents but the wild act of sex their parents were engaged in.

Shocked and horrified, the children let out an ear-piercing squeal in unison, dropped the fancy tray of breakfast goodies onto the floor, ran into the kitchen to gather their wits, and leaned over the sink to wash the disturbing visions out of their eyeballs. Young Luke declared, "I don't know what they were doing in there, but whatever it was, it looked like Dad was winning."

Yes, it is every parent's nightmare—being discovered in an incredibly intimate and vulnerable position by none other than your own offspring. I think it is safe to say that it is every *child's* nightmare as well. One man told me that as a preschooler, he entered his parents' room one night feeling sick. But his mom and dad were completely oblivious to his presence and continued their sexual play. Upon realizing their son was standing in their bedroom, the father leaped from the bed, grabbed his pants off the floor, slid the leather belt out of the belt loops, and began swinging wildly to punish the boy for his "voyeurism."

With tears in his eyes, this grown man explained, "I didn't

even know what voyeurism was . . . or what they were doing under the covers . . . nor did I really care. I just knew I needed their attention. It was the most traumatic moment of my life to be beaten with a belt by such an angry father when I didn't even understand what he was so angry about."

Even more disturbing was to hear that when this man grew old enough (during his teen years) to realize what they had been doing in bed that night, he automatically and erroneously assumed that sex was something that one *needed* to feel guilty and embarrassed about—and something that needed to be kept entirely secret, even if it meant using anger and violence to protect those secrets.

You can imagine the kind of impact these messages had on his sexual development. Even with his wife of thirty years, he struggled with negative, shameful feelings about all things sexual. And he didn't feel any freedom whatsoever to discuss sexuality with anyone—not his wife, not his children, not his pastor, or any friend. Fortunately he came to a marriage conference where my husband and I spoke, and his emotional floodgates burst wide open during a private session we had with him and his wife. It is an overwhelming experience to see forty-five-year-old tears about such a painful childhood experience flowing from a fifty-year-old man, but I was grateful to witness God reveal the *root* of his sexual insecurities and begin the healing process in his life and marriage.

As weird as it may sound, I left that session thankful that my parents alluded to their sex life just often enough for me to grow up knowing that it is very normal for married couples to be physically intimate. Sure, it turned my stomach to see them petting and flirting with each other on occasion, but in hindsight, it was one of the biggest favors they could have done for their children—to show us that marriage *is* the place where sexual intimacy can be freely enjoyed.

As I first began speaking on the topic of healthy sexuality back in the 1990s, it was usually to teenage youth groups. Without fail, when I would explain the mechanics of sex, there would always be at least one kid in the group who would insist, "No way! My parents don't do *that!*"

I would challenge them, asking what gave them the impression that their parents didn't have sex. Their response is worth noting by all of us parents. They would rebut: "My mom and dad don't even kiss, or hold hands, or go out on dates. What makes you think they have sex?"

That is a hard argument to press back against.

And with teenagers who assume that their parents *don't* have sex, guess what their attitude about their own sexuality usually becomes? "If I'm going to have good, hot sex, I'd better do it *now* while I'm single because when I get married, I'm probably *not* getting any." After all, they have seen many of those sitcoms and movies featuring the frigid wife holding out on the sexually frustrated husband. But it's not just the media that teaches kids about marital sex (or lack thereof). Sadly, this message is often reinforced in the home.

I tell you these stories to warn you that, yes, children will at times present challenges to your sex life, such as when your toddler is running a fever and needs to sleep directly between Mom and Dad, when you have to stay up until all hours of the night to help your elementary school student with her science project, or when your teenager declares to you at 11 p.m., just as you are settling into your spouse's arms, "But I need you to quiz me for my exam tomorrow!" (like my own son did the night before I wrote this). Those are moments when you simply have to table your testosterone, slide out of your satin sheets, slip on your super-parent cape, and focus on being *their* hero.

But I also want to assure you that raising children doesn't have to be the end of your passionate lovemaking, nor should it be. Again, our children need to grow up with an understanding that marriage is the relationship where great sex can be thoroughly enjoyed.

> Our children need to grow up with an understanding that marriage is the relationship where great sex can be thoroughly enjoyed.

The generations before ours had this concept down pat. For example, my grandparents grew up in tiny homes, where Mom and Dad's sleeping quarters were often just a corner of the one-room house, separated from the rest of the family by a burlap-sack curtain. No soundproof walls or locked doors meant that the children grew up knowing that parents do pretty much the same things that the farm animals do on a daily basis. No secrets. No shame. No shock necessary. It just was what it was. And as awkward as it may have been at times, it served a beautiful purpose—to pass the baton of healthy sexuality within marriage from one generation to the next.

We have lost that in today's society, relegating our parental sex-educator role to peers, Internet porn, public school systems, trashy TV shows, and silver screen celebrities who certainly do *not* share our Christian values about sexuality. I am not advocating that you tear down your soundproof walls, put a screen door on your bedroom, or make sex a public affair around your house. But I am saying that your sex life does not—I repeat, *does not*—have to suffer just because you have children dwelling under the same roof. It is perfectly okay to claim a parental time-out a few times per week for you to enjoy some *quiet time* together in the privacy of your own bedroom and for your kids to know that sexual intimacy takes place behind that closed door. And they can look forward to that same dynamic someday when they are married.

Thankfully I heard a speaker present a similar message when our children were pretty young. So as soon as they were old enough to comprehend (around three or four years old), we explained, "You know how sometimes you like to have Mommy all to yourself? And sometimes you want time with Daddy all to yourself? Well, sometimes mommies and daddies like to have each other all to themselves, without children in the middle. So sometimes we're going to go into our room to spend special time together alone, and we'll put in a Barney tape for you. Just watch your movie or read a book, but don't come knocking unless there is blood or vomit, okay?"

Our children grew up with the full understanding that parents spend time alone together. And when they were old enough to know where babies come from and how they are made, we explained what parents do behind those closed doors. And they didn't blush or bat an eyelash. There simply has never been any shame in our household surrounding sexuality, and we do not want there ever to be any. We knew those cute little babies we brought home from the hospital would be sexual beings from cradle to grave, just like we are. So there never has been a need to ignore the elephant in the living room. We have talked about all kinds of sexual topics at every stage of our children's development. We want to equip them with the tools they need to be good stewards of their sexuality. It is simply too precious of a gift to squander out of ignorance because parents are too embarrassed to talk about it.

Which reminds me of a day when my son, a junior high student at the time, came knocking on our bedroom door. We responded with the standard, "We'll be out in a little while!" Once I finally emerged from our room and began walking out to my car for something, he began walking alongside me with a big grin on his face. I said, "Matthew, what is your deal?"

"I know what you guys were doing in there," he smirked.

I decided to play along and said, "Oh, yeah? And are *you* looking forward to doing that when *you* have a wife someday?" (Yes, I believe I shocked him when I didn't try to deny his suspicion.)

"Well, yeah!" he declared unapologetically. But then his look of enthusiasm evolved into a look of disgust as he added, "But not yet!"

And I couldn't have hoped for a more appropriate response.

PONDER THE PRINCIPLE

- How did your parents teach you about healthy sexuality? How effective was their strategy?
- What would you like to do differently in educating your own children about their sexuality?
- On another sheet of paper list three things you will

do as parents to instill healthy sexual values in your children and approximately the right time to do those things with each of them, based on their ages.

Let Freedom Ring!

37. IS THE "MISSIONARY POSITION" THE ONLY "HOLY" WAY TO HAVE SEX?

GROWING UP, MY MOM WENT TO THE GROCERY STORE EVERY Friday afternoon and purchased roughly the same items each week, one of which was a quart of vanilla ice cream packaged in a rectangular, blue cardboard container. For years dessert in our household usually consisted of a bowlful of vanilla ice cream and a handful of cookies on the side.

Then one day, my uncle Tommy and aunt Brenda came to Greenville, Texas, for a visit and took us to a place I never had been before—the Sabine Valley Ice Cream Shop. I wondered why we were going "out" for ice cream when we had some in the freezer, but eager to tag along, I gathered my Holly Hobby doll and hand-crocheted purse and set out on the adventure.

Imagine my surprise when I walked in and discovered freezer cases with multiple cardboard barrels containing a w-i-d-e variety of ice cream flavors. Sure, they had vanilla, but they also had vanilla with cookies already crunched up and swirled in, vanilla laced with ribbons of caramel and chocolate fudge, and vanilla sprinkled with gummy bears throughout. And there were dozens of other flavors featuring everything from marshmallows to malted milk balls, from coconut to candy bar pieces, from pistachios to praline pecans. There was even one flavor with an entire rainbow of different sherbets all in the same barrel. I was overwhelmed by the choices, but I remember picking one called homemade peach. Yes, it was divine. And I believed that surely there were many other divine flavors just waiting to be sampled.

So the Sabine Valley Ice Cream Shop became one of our favorite outings, and I looked forward to trying a *new* flavor each time. Never again would I settle for the same old thing when a whole new world of flavors was awaiting me.

Variety *is* the spice of life. Variety adds a little sparkle to our eye, and a little pep in our step that keeps us from settling into comfortable ruts. If this is true, then why do we so often settle into certain sexual ruts—particularly the rut of engaging in the exact same sexual position over and over as if *vanilla* sex is all there is? Most likely because, somewhere along the way, many of us Christians believed the myth that the "missionary position" was the only "holy" way to have sex.

The phrase *missionary position* is believed to have been coined by sex researcher Dr. Alfred Kinsey back in the 1940s when he was working on his book *Sexual Behavior in the Human Male*. Kinsey theorized that Christian missionaries were responsible for teaching people that the "face-to-face, man on top, woman on bottom" sexual position was the only "pure" way of having sex although there is debate as to whether or not this is actually true.[1] Regardless of how the term was coined, it is interesting what a huge cultural phenomenon the holiness of the missionary position has created. I think it might rank right up there on the biggest-myths ladder along with "the world is flat," and "if you touch yourself 'down there,' you'll grow hair on your palms, go blind, and become a pencil salesman."

But is the missionary position really the only holy way of having sex in marriage? I seriously doubt it, based on the following reasons:

- The Bible in no way suggests that God holds this preference for how His people engage in sexual intimacy. In fact, numerous passages in the Song of Solomon indicate that God celebrates a variety of positions in the marriage bed.
- Proponents suggest that the missionary position is the only way that a couple can have sex face-to-face. This is simply not true. A woman can be on top and still be face-to-face with her husband, and a couple can be side by side in somewhat of a "scissor" position (legs intertwined to allow penetration) and still be face-to-face.
- Some insist that human beings are the only species that God created that can have sex face-to-face, so that is their responsibility. I hate to burst anyone's evolutionary bubble, but armadillos can only have sex face-to-face. Humpback whales and dolphins can only have sex face-to-face. Bonobo monkeys often have sex face-to-face. It is a sweet sentiment to say that human beings are unique in this way, but it just doesn't hold water.

But do you know what theory *does* hold water? That human beings are entirely free to engage in any sexual position that is comfortable and pleasurable to both partners. I don't care who is on top or what body part is touching what body part. It is all holy. It is all God's creation. It is all divinely inspired when a husband and wife take great delight in one another's bodies. If you just particularly *enjoy* the missionary position, and you prefer to do it that way every time you make love, then more power to you! Seriously, that is completely a couple's prerogative. I am not saying you *have to* experiment with a variety of positions; I am simply saying that you *can* if you so choose.

So before you buy the lie that there is only *one* proper way to have sex and all the rest is sin, remember that there is *freedom* in the marriage bed—freedom to enjoy each other until our hearts (and bodies) are completely content. We do not need to fear judgment from the God who gave us such a strong sex drive and appetite for variety in the first place.

In fact, I would like you to consider for a moment how I believe God really feels about this topic, so join me for a little visualization exercise. Let's pretend that an incredibly wealthy king gives each of his grown children his or her own house to live in. Not just any house, but each dwelling has been custom-tailored to each child's personality and tastes. He has a beautiful English cottage built for his daughter, landscaped with trumpet vines, lavender bushes, and all sorts of other flowering plants and trees, and a cobblestone path meanders through an orchard of succulent fruit trees. For his son, he has a grand log cabin built on the side of a mountain, with a large deck overlooking a pristine fishing pond. Both son and daughter are set to enjoy a lifetime in these luxurious surroundings.

But one day the king is strolling through the city streets and stumbles unexpectedly upon his son and daughter dressed in rags and crouching inside a cardboard box. Bewildered, the king inquires, "What are you doing here in the streets like homeless people? Why aren't you enjoying the houses I had built for you?"

The son and daughter reply, "Well, those houses are indeed amazing, but we were afraid that if we enjoyed them too much, you might, uh, judge us."

Can you imagine the king's shock? His dismay? His utter disbelief? Why in the world would these adult children presume that their father would judge them for enjoying something that he fully intended for their pleasure? Why would they choose to limit their existence to a cardboard box when so many delights are awaiting them in their own extravagant homes?

> Instead of fearing God's judgment if we enjoy these sexual bodies *too much*, we should fear His disappointment if we *don't*.

Do you make the connection between this scenario and the sexual bodies God has given us to live in? He has gone to such great lengths, designing us such that we can experience incredible physical pleasures throughout life. Why would we choose *not* to enjoy them? So, perhaps, instead of fearing God's judgment if we enjoy these sexual bodies *too much*, we should fear His disappointment if we *don't*.

38. WHAT ABOUT ORAL OR ANAL SEX IN MARRIAGE?

In high school I was sitting in the bleachers, having a conversation with some senior girls, and as is often the case, the topic rolled around to sex. One girl mentioned oral sex specifically, although I don't remember in what context. Another girl's face grew rather perplexed, and we could almost smell smoke coming out of her ears as if there was a lot going on in her brain at the moment. Someone asked, "Amy, is something wrong?"

"What *is* oral sex exactly?" Amy inquired, to which someone responded with an explanation that one partner's genitals are stimulated by the other partner's mouth. Amy's jaw dropped, and she looked rather disgusted. We all got a big kick out of it when she was finally able to speak and proclaimed, "Oh, gee! I thought oral sex meant just talking sexy to each other." Yeah, not exactly!

Then a few years later, when I was a youth pastor, we had taken our senior high students on a sexuality retreat weekend, hoping to instill an appreciation for the concept of remaining sexually abstinent until marriage. Of course, the question of oral sex came up, this time from a guy. When I explained the physical mechanics of such, one sixteen-year-old girl looked at her mother (who was chaperoning the event) and asked out loud in front of everyone, "You and Dad don't do *that*, do you?" (Yes, I made a big, fat mental note in that moment: *Create a rule that disallows any teen from asking adults intimate questions about their private sex lives, especially in a public setting!* We live and learn, don't we?) The mom, not wanting to lie, simply responded, "Well, babe, freedom in the marriage bed!" Her daughter's face turned an interesting shade of green, and she ran off to the bathroom to toss her cookies. Fifteen years later the daughter is now married herself and laughs hysterically at her own response back then.

Do you recall the first time you ever heard about oral sex? What was your response? Were you grossed out or curious? And what about now that you are married? Is this an act you are comfortable with or not? The most common questions I receive about oral sex are (1) is it acceptable outside of marriage, and (2) is it a sin inside of marriage?

My personal opinion is that it should *not* be an acceptable

CELEBRATE THE PHYSICAL SIDE OF SEX

practice outside of marriage. After all, it is called oral *sex* for a reason. It is far too personal and intimate of an act for two people who are not married to each other to engage in, and it creates all kinds of temptations to take things one step farther to intercourse. Does that mean that all Christian couples make it to the altar without having indulged in this type of foreplay? Probably not. But I still think it is wise to save such an intimate act until vows have been exchanged. Once vows are exchanged, then we can view oral sex through a completely different lens.

Some couples choose not to engage in oral sex at all, for varying reasons, and I respect that completely. After all, there *is* freedom in the marriage bed, meaning that you can do just about anything that you both are comfortable with (as long as Scripture does not forbid it), but that does not necessarily mean that you have to. No one should ever have to do anything sexually that he or she perceives negatively. I don't take any issue whatsoever with a couple who chooses to refrain from a certain sexual activity. If they both feel the same way about it, then there is nothing broken, therefore, nothing to fix.

But what about when one partner wants oral sex and the other does not? What then? As we discussed earlier, the one who desires something sexually should always submit to the one who has an aversion to it, as trust and genuine intimacy would be destroyed otherwise. But I also think that sometimes we need to be willing to experiment with something that we know would bring our partners great pleasure. After all, we are the only ones ordained by God to provide sexual pleasure to our spouses, so hopefully we can become comfortable offering them every healthy sexual satisfaction.

My suggestion is to openly discuss the reasons behind why you both feel the way you do, positive and negative. For those who have concerns, you may find some irrational beliefs that drive such negativity. For example, some coaching clients are not comfortable with oral sex because . . .

- they fear displeasing God
- they don't think it is "natural"
- they believe it to be a "dirty" act

Let's address these concerns one at a time. Should we fear displeasing God by engaging in oral sex within the context of a marriage relationship? I think we can trust Scripture to guide us in this regard. If God took issue with it, He surely would have spelled that out in His instruction manual. Although the Bible does not use the term *oral sex*, it is alluded to quite vividly in many passages throughout the Song of Solomon, such as . . .

Like the finest apple tree in the orchard
    is my lover among other young men.
I sit in his delightful shade
    and taste his delicious fruit.
He escorts me to the banquet hall;
    it's obvious how much he loves me. . . .

Awake, north wind!
    Rise up, south wind!
Blow on my garden
    and spread its fragrance all around.

> Come into your garden, my love;
>> taste its finest fruits. . . .

> His mouth is sweetness itself;
>> he is desirable in every way.
>> (Song of Songs 2:3–4; 4:16; 5:16)

In case you didn't catch it, "sitting in her lover's shade" implies that he is standing over her, and she is tasting his "fruit." Bible scholars believe the term *fruit* to be a poetic reference to the genitals. Therefore, this sounds a lot like oral sex to me. In addition, the passage requesting that her lover "blow on my garden" and "taste its choice fruits" is also believed to be a reference to oral-genital contact, as the term *garden* is a poetic reference to the female genitals.

However, the Song of Songs is intended to be a descriptive book, not a prescriptive book. The writer is not saying that all married people must do this. He is merely saying there is freedom to indulge in this activity as they feel the passion and desire to do so. It is okay if you *do not* feel that desire, but I think it would be more honest and God-honoring simply to say, "I personally don't care for oral sex." To say, "Surely God doesn't approve of oral sex" is simply nothing short of heresy.

The next reason often cited for refusing to engage in oral sex is that it is not "natural." If we really stop to consider how God intended a married couple to engage in intercourse, we have to acknowledge that there must be lubrication in order to make the act comfortable and pleasurable. But there are some seasons of a woman's life where the well naturally runs a little dry. How did God intend to compensate for that? K-Y Jelly was not invented until 1904. Astroglide did not appear on store shelves until 1982. So what have couples done for centuries prior? I believe God designed the most effective lubricant ever known to man—human saliva, which is far better than K-Y Jelly or Astroglide. That's right; saliva is not just to help us digest food. It also aids in sexual activity. It never gets gloppy or sticky. It doesn't change the pH balance of a woman's vaginal area or cause yeast to multiply. It simply creates enough moisture to allow sex to be pleasurable. And you never have to remember to pack it for a trip. It is always handy, always just "on the tip of your tongue."

And let's be real. To those who are comfortable with the concept, oral sex provides an enormous amount of pleasure to both male and female recipients. It is one of the most common forms of sexual foreplay for a very good reason—it primes the pump sexually like nothing else. Plus, most husbands and wives who enjoy the practice declare that oral sex can also be a very pleasurable, loving act to perform.

The final reason sometimes quoted is because some consider oral sex to be a "dirty" act. Sometimes this belief comes from having been sexually abused as a child, where oral sex was forced in an inappropriate relationship, so, of course, it felt dirty. In such a violent or manipulative context, it is. But marriage is another story altogether. Your spouse is your sexual partner, not your sexual abuser. I suggest you talk with a therapist who can help you overcome the negative associations you may have regarding oral sex, which often include nausea, gag reflexes, or other psychosomatic issues. There are several exercises that can be implemented to help desensitize you to such negative responses, so there is hope if oral sex is something you aspire to enjoy.

Then again, being sexually abused may have nothing to do

CELEBRATE THE PHYSICAL SIDE OF SEX

with it at all. For some, it is a germ issue. While everyone is enti-
tled to their own opinion, the notion that human genitals are not
designed by God to be orally stimulated due to health hazards
does not hold water with most doctors. Do the penis and vagina
need to be properly cleansed in order for the spouse to have a
pleasant experience while performing oral sex? Certainly. That
is a given. Nobody wants to put their mouth somewhere that has
not been washed recently. And we are also assuming there is no
active sexually transmitted disease present, such as herpes, which
can be transmitted from genitals to mouth, and vice versa. But in
the absence of any disease or poor hygiene, there is no reason not
to pleasure your partner orally if both of you so desire. Medically
speaking, it is just as "dirty" (or "germ-spreading") to passionately
kiss someone as it is to engage in oral sex, yet most of us don't let
the presence of those germs stop us from kissing our spouses as
often as we want.

With anal sex, however, I do believe there are medical issues,
and I am far more concerned about it from a medical perspective than from a spiritual perspective. Why? Believe it or not,
anal sex appears to be forbidden in Scripture only between two
males. Linda Dillow and Lorraine Pintus write in their book
Intimate Issues:

> In the Old Testament, sodomy refers to men lying with men.
> The English word means "Unnatural sexual intercourse,
> especially of one man with another or of a human being with
> an animal." Unfortunately some Christian teachers have
> erroneously equated sodomy with anal sex. In the Bible, sod-
> omites refer to male homosexuals, or temple prostitutes (both
> male and female). In contemporary usage, the term *sodomy* is

sometimes used to describe anal intercourse between a man and woman. This is not the meaning of the biblical word.[2]

Therefore, we cannot say, "Anal sex between a consenting husband and wife in the context of marriage is a sin—thus saith the Lord!" Sorry, but God did not say that. But He did give us each a brain, and common sense tells us that just because something is not expressly forbidden in Scripture does not mean it is a perfectly healthy practice. I personally believe it to be a very *unhealthy* practice, and many other experts concur. In his book *A Celebration of Sex*, Dr. Doug Rosenau makes the following statement about anal sex:

> The vaginal tissue, with its lubrication and muscle, was designed for childbirth and intercourse, but the anus was not. The anus was meant to push out waste, not sustain vigorous thrusting. With hemorrhoids and the fragility of the rectal tissue, it is better not to make it an organ of sexual play. Also, the many bacteria in the anus can interfere with the bacterial balance in the vagina and cause infections.[3]

Because of these undeniable medical truths, Dr. Rosenau encourages men to "forget the [anal sex] obsessions that could potentially wreck an otherwise healthy sex life." I couldn't agree more.

The anus is designed for one-way traffic—for things to exit but not to enter. Since the perineum is such a sexually sensitive area, however, some women enjoy oral or digital foreplay just around the opening of the anus. As long as proper hygiene has been made a priority, it's okay if her husband wants to linger around that exit door, as long as nothing fully enters this sensitive area. The same can be said for men as well. Stimulation of the external part of the anus may be fine if his wife is game, but internal anal stimulation is something I discourage for obvious health reasons.

Dear Jesus, far be it from us to do anything sexually that would harm one another or endanger each other's physical health. Give us the wisdom to guard ourselves against anything that wouldn't be beneficial in our marriage bed and the courage to freely and fully enjoy anything that would bring us closer together sexually and spiritually. Amen.

39. WHAT ABOUT SEX TOYS IN MARRIAGE?[4]

With all of this talk about freedom to experience all kinds of sexual pleasures in the marriage bed, our conversations wouldn't be complete without acknowledging that sometimes the word *orgasm* is easier said than done. There are some couples who have tried multiple times and multiple ways to pleasure one another to the point of climax but find their efforts fall short of the goal. But all is not lost simply because a couple needs a little help. There are marital aids that can spark a whole new level of interest, arousal, and yes, even climax if you are willing to let go of your inhibitions and give them a try.

Since a woman can require several minutes of clitoral or vaginal stimulation in order to reach orgasm (twenty to forty minutes isn't unusual), she may benefit from a little help from a (battery-powered) friend. Some husbands don't mind participating in sexual marathons and have strong fingers, tongues, and erections with which to do so. Others may find it a little tedious or too exhausting to participate in such a marathon very frequently. But with the help of a marital aid, it can be a win-win experience for both spouses.

Perhaps at this moment everything within you is screaming, "I can't believe she is talking about this stuff!" If the idea of owning a vibrator or marital aid is so offensive to you, then don't own one. I repeat: *Don't own one!* I am not prescribing them for all couples but merely describing them for those who may find these very items to be just the boost they need to add sizzle to their sex lives or overcome their physical sexual hurdles. I recognize that there may be a few mental obstacles to being the proud owner of a marital aid, so let's look at some of the ideas that may be rolling around in your mind.

- *Surely God doesn't approve of marital aids in the marriage bed!* Actually, there is absolutely no place in Scripture that states, "Thou shalt not have a battery-powered orgasm." If something as simple as a sex toy brings a married couple together in the bedroom far more often, I can't imagine God doesn't smile upon that.
- *I don't want my husband to feel threatened by a vibrator.* Before you jump to the conclusion that your husband *would* feel threatened by a vibrator, have you discussed it with him? In my dealings with married couples, marital aids are often a welcome friend because they level the playing field and help him overcome his own fears. What fears am I talking about? The fear that his wife will think he is selfish because they only have ten minutes and he wants sex, but she requires at least twenty minutes of stimulation to experience

an orgasm . . . so what is a guy to do? Squelch his own
desires? Run the risk of offending her by expecting a one-
sided encounter?

Honestly, some men react very positively to the idea
of having a marital aid that can speed up the process or
increase her arousal when necessary. In fact, vibrators can
send a woman over the edge almost as fast, if not faster,
than a man experiences ejaculation. If he can enlist the help
of a marital aid when needed or desired, he may feel the
freedom to initiate sex much more often, feeling confident
that he can pleasure his wife as fully as he wants to be
pleasured himself. Also, it is much more fun for a man to
have sex with a woman who is enjoying herself. If a vibrator
is all it takes to turn sex from a marital duty into a mind-
blowing experience for both of you, isn't it worth it?

• *I don't want to get spoiled to the strong sensations of a vibrator
and begin to prefer that over intimacy with my husband.* This
is an honorable sentiment, and if it is working for you,
great! If you are experiencing wonderful orgasms as often
as you would like, and he is not feeling in the least bit
overwhelmed by what it takes to get you there, then you
probably don't need a vibrator. But if fear that you would
prefer the battery-powered sensations over your husband's
touch is the only thing holding you back, let me paint a new
picture for you. Why does it have to be *either/or*? Why can't
it be *both/and*? Why do you feel that you would abandon
one for the other, when you could be enjoying both? Keep
in mind that ideally (at least in my opinion), vibrators are
to be used as a "marital aid," not a "masturbation aid." If
you agree, create a rule that says it is not for individual

play but, rather, to enhance the playtimes you have *together*. Besides, ladies, you would not be the only one who enjoys the good vibrations. Marital aids can be just as effective at stimulating men as they are women.

- *I don't want to look at all the pornographic stuff in catalogs or on websites in order to shop for such products, and I'm certainly not going to walk into a XXX bookstore to buy one in person!* Again, honorable sentiment. I prefer not to look at pornography either, nor do I care to be seen walking out of an adult toy store with a plain brown paper bag full of who-knows-what. Sex is personal. It is private. And it is a beautiful means of reinforcing a married couple's healthy relationship. But, granted, so much of what you encounter when shopping for marital aids is anything but beautiful or edifying to a Christian married couple. That is why I recommend a company called Covenant Spice (www.covenantspice .com). They carry all the latest and greatest marital aids and intimacy-enhancing products, but you are shown only the products themselves, not people using them. It is all good, clean, marriage-building fun at Covenant Spice. They even have a satisfaction guarantee and very discreet shipping, which leads us to the next possible concern.

- *What would the kids think if they found our sex toy?* I can understand the desire to protect children from such discoveries. But if we can be crafty enough to successfully keep the box of expensive gourmet chocolates safely hidden somewhere in the kitchen, I would think we can be crafty enough to keep a marital toy box locked and safely hidden somewhere in the master bedroom or closet. There are even specially designed cases with combination locks for such a purpose. But even if the toy box was found—is it really wrong for a married couple to own it? Is it a crime to want the best sex life possible with the person to whom you have committed your life? Absolutely not. One woman admitted to me recently, "My mother never talked to me about sex, but finding her vibrator in her lingerie drawer was the best nonverbal lesson in sexual freedom I think she could have given me." After the shock wears off, realizing that our parents are also sexual beings can give us complete freedom to embrace our sexuality as well.

I want to reiterate again that I am not saying that all couples should own a marital aid. Please do not send me letters and e-mails saying how disgraceful it is that I would even suggest the use of sex toys. Just hear my heart when I say that if you need a marital aid to overcome any sexual challenges, you do not have to apologize to anyone for it. You do not have to fill out a legal form to acquire a permit for one. Nor do you have to approach your spiritual leader and schedule a time for confession over the matter. There is freedom in the marriage bed! If you *need* one, or if you simply *desire* one, don't let society's sexual taboos rob you of your peace of mind in owning one.

Shannon's Question to *You*

40. WHERE IS YOUR "FINISH LINE"?

I AM SO BLESSED TO RECEIVE FREQUENT E-MAILS AND LETTERS about the impact that my books or speaking engagements have had on someone's life and marriage. As I close this book, I could not imagine a more appropriate encouragement to couples than to share the following letter from Helen, which made my husband and me do triple backflips—both for her and for her husband as well. Helen's name has been changed to protect her identity, as I feel certain she would not want her whole church knowing these intimate details of her sex life, but I am honored that she shared them with me, and based on what she has written, I believe she wants me to share them with *you* as well. Helen wrote:

> Shannon, you spoke at our church this past year. I was one of the "older" gals in the crowd. My husband and I have been married almost fifty years, and we're probably considered the poster children for the "happily married couple." I wanted to share what happened to me at the retreat.
>
> I prayed that Friday morning that the Lord would use me

and that I would be open to anything He wanted to teach me. Then I went off to the retreat. And then you showed up . . .

If anyone had asked me, I would have said that my husband and I have a great sex life and have from the beginning of our marriage. I had orgasms easily from the first day of our marriage. We are fortunate in that we were both virgins and believers when we got married. . . . I thought our sex life was "normal" and better than most. Yes, my husband seemed to want it all the time, and yes, I was worn out during the child-rearing season so we did have plenty of those "not tonight" discussions during those years. But I was always happy to "pay" him for help around the house with a "quickie" every so often.

So what happened at the retreat?

I keep asking myself that question. Something *major* happened. My menopause lasted many years, and I had several health issues and enough depression to warrant medication. Unfortunately a side effect of the medication was that I could no longer have an orgasm. Having never had that problem before, I begged God for the feeling to come back, to the point of tears, but eventually told God that I would be content with whatever I currently had or did not have. I stopped the anti-depressants after a few months, but the ability to climax never returned. My husband has also had some erectile dysfunction issues over the past decade, but we've operated under the premise that it's always too soon to give up! This has resulted in greater intimacy. Even though all we had to offer each other sometimes was holding and kissing, we never gave up wanting all we could have with one another.

So what happened at the retreat? Over twenty years ago my husband approached me about doing a little more experimenting. By that he meant he wanted to have oral sex. I was dead-set against it. It just seemed wrong to me. I tried to explain that intimacy to me was face-to-face, mouth to mouth, etc. We tried it a few times but I hated it and finally asked him not to bring it up again. He graciously complied. I mention all of this for two reasons: 1) a person's mental attitude is everything, and 2) as I have thought about this over the past few days, I believe my husband's selflessness and not-insisting attitude communicated that he loved and respected me, and that however I felt about something was all right. He wanted to please me more than he wanted to please himself. I believe his wonderful attitude contributed to the freedom that I experienced after your retreat.

Somehow, by God's grace and the anointing on what you say and how you say it, God did something amazing. I'm not sure what He did or if I even know which time you spoke or if it was an accumulation of what you said plus your book. But it was like I had a curtain over my mind and suddenly God pulled the curtain back and set me free to fully enjoy myself! Though I had heard and believed the saying that "nothing is wrong between you and your mate if it is all right with both of you," somehow, I now had a new green light that God made these parts of our bodies for our enjoyment. More to the point, it was all right for me to enjoy it all! In fact, God delights in me enjoying myself!

My husband said I was different when I walked in the door after the retreat. I am free and I can't explain it except that God has done something marvelous! I came home and started reading your books out loud to my husband. I got online and ordered some "special aids" from the Christian website you recommended. Thank you for that. Wow! They have really helped. We are having a summer of romance, for sure! Except for when he's out of town, we have only missed one day of sex since the retreat! We've even done it three times in one day! I have even begun having orgasms again for the first time in twenty years, and I have high hopes for many more to come! (Pardon the pun!)

I felt I wanted to write to you, Shannon, because I want women to know that it is never too late to more fully enjoy one's mate! (Even if she thinks she's already enjoying him!) I'm also telling you these very private things about us because the devil really loves to lie to people my age that "some things are over" and I would like for older couples to be encouraged otherwise.

I told my husband the other day that often I feel like I am this special child that God so loves. I was walking along, minding my own business, showed up at the retreat expecting to be a blessing to others, but not even suspecting the great gift He was about to give me, or how much more fun was ahead of me/us! I love God. He is amazing and loves us so much. I have been surprised by this overwhelming joy and I can't thank my heavenly Father enough.

I can't thank you enough either, Shannon. Thank you, thank you, thank you! We believe you have a special anointing to talk about sexuality to all ages. God bless you for doing what He has gifted you to do. We are also reading *Every Young Woman's Battle* because we're sending copies to our granddaughters. I can't wait to discuss the book with them when we're together!

Rejoicing,
Helen

We rejoice with you, too, Helen! Hooray for you for realizing that our marriage beds can continue to be verdant (Song of Songs 1:16 NIV) long into our golden years!

Our sexual pilot lights do not have to go out completely just because we reach a certain age. They can always be reignited as long as there is breath in our lungs and blood circulating in our bodies. And oh, what pleasures *still* await us—especially when we open ourselves to celebrating the fantastic freedom, intense pleasure, and absolute euphoria that God intends for us to enjoy in the marriage bed.

You may not be at the point in your life yet when you are worried about remaining sexually active as you age. Perhaps you are still in the first decade or two of marriage and trying to figure out how to further open lines of communication about your sexual desires and expectations. Maybe kids and careers and domestic life crowd out the time and energy you once had for sexual intimacy, and you are just trying to figure out how to stay connected in spite of the chaos. Or maybe you have been married long enough that you feel as if you have tried everything, and you are looking for ways to keep things interesting in the bedroom.

We all are in different seasons and in different ages and stages of our lives. But the one thing we all have in common—regardless of age, gender, or any other factor—is that we are *sexual* beings, created by God for sexual connection.

My prayer is that by embracing these passion principles—by embracing the spiritual, mental, emotional, and physical facets of our sexuality—you will have the powerful tools in your marital tool belt to create many moments of passion and pleasure for many years to come. Keep talking together . . . keep praying together . . . keep touching each other . . . and keep celebrating the sexual freedom we have in marriage!

PONDER THE PRINCIPLE

- Where do you envision your "finish line" to be? Will you let age dictate when your sex life is over? Why or why not?
- What are the physical and mental benefits to maintaining a healthy sex life for as long as possible?
- Do you think there might be emotional and spiritual benefits to sexual intimacy between an aging couple? If so, describe them.
- What are you looking most forward to about growing old together?

Notes

PASSION PRINCIPLE #1:
CELEBRATE THE SPIRITUAL SIDE OF SEX

ONE + ONE = ONE

1. Raymond Collins, "The Bible and Sexuality," *Biblical Theology Bulletin* 7 (1977): 153, quoted in Richard M. Davidson, "The Theology of Sexuality in the Beginning: Genesis 1–2," *Andrews University Seminary Studies* 26, no. 1 (Spring 1998): 2, http://www.bibelschule.info/streaming/Richard-M.-Davidson---The-Theology-of-Sexuality-in-the-Beginning---Genesis-1-2_24058.pdf.

2. Richard M. Davidson, "The Theology of Sexuality in the Beginning: Genesis 1–2," *Andrews University Seminary Studies* 26, no. 1 (Spring 1998): 2, http://www.bibelschule.info/streaming/Richard-M.-Davidson---The-Theology-of-Sexuality-in-the-Beginning---Genesis-1-2_24058.pdf.

3. This quote is widely attributed to former U.S. surgeon general C. Everett Koop. Author accessed the quote on May 10, 2013, at http://www.lifelinepcc.org/abstinence.html.

THE *GENESIS* OF SEX

1. *Disciple's Study Bible, New International Version* (Nashville: Holman Bible Publishers, 1988), 802.

2. Peter Kreeft, *Everything You Ever Wanted to Know About Heaven—but Never Dreamed of Asking* (San Francisco: Ignatius,

1990), 117–18. See www.peterkreeft.com/topics/sex-in-heaven. htm for an excerpt, "Is There Sex in Heaven?"

THE GOSPEL TRUTH

1. Shannon Ethridge, *Completely His: Loving Jesus Without Limits* (Colorado Springs: WaterBrook, 2008).
2. *Merriam-Webster's Online Dictionary,* s.v. "passion," accessed April 22, 2013, http://www.merriam-webster.com/dictionary/passion.
3. James B. Nelson, *The Intimate Connection: Male Sexuality, Masculine Spirituality* (Philadelphia: Westminster, 1988), 13–14.
4. *Wikibooks,* s.v. "Galatians 5," accessed May 10, 2013, http://en.wikibooks.org/wiki/Biblical_Studies/New_Testament_Commentaries/Galatians/Chapter_5.
5. Charles Henderson, "Sexuality and Spirituality: A Sacramental View of Sex," GodWeb.org, www.godweb.org/sexspirit.htm.
6. Shannon Ethridge, *The Fantasy Fallacy: Exposing the Deeper Meaning Behind Sexual Thoughts* (Nashville: Thomas Nelson, 2012), 100.
7. Peter Kreeft, *Everything You Ever Wanted to Know About Heaven—but Never Dreamed of Asking* (San Francisco: Ignatius, 1990). See www.peterkreeft.com/topics/sex-in-heaven.htm for an excerpt, "Is There Sex in Heaven?"

PLAYING BY THE RULE BOOK

1. Stephen Arterburn and Fred Stoeker, *Every Man's Marriage: An Every Man's Guide to Winning the Heart of a Woman* (Colorado Springs: WaterBrook, 2010), 273–74.

PASSION PRINCIPLE #2:
CELEBRATE THE MENTAL SIDE OF SEX

SEX ON THE BRAIN

1. Louann Brizendine, *The Female Brain* (New York: Bantam, 2008), 127.
2. Ibid., 125.

3. Ibid., 105.
4. Ibid., 101.
5. Ibid., 134, 144.

RULES OF (MENTAL) ENGAGEMENT
1. Luke Gilkerson, *Your Brain on Porn*, 3, http://www.covenanteyes .com/brain-ebook.
2. Gary R. Brooks, *The Centerfold Syndrome: How Men Can Overcome Objectification and Achieve Intimacy with Women* (San Francisco: Jossey-Bass, 1995), 2–11.
3. Naomi Wolf, "The Porn Myth," *New York*, October 20, 2003, http://nymag.com/nymetro/news/trends/n_9437/.
4. Gilkerson, *Your Brain on Porn*, 7–8.
5. Dolf Zillmann, "Influence of unrestrained access to erotic on adolescents' and young adults' disposition toward sexuality," *Journal of Adolescent Health* 27, no. 2, supplement 1, 2000.
6. Safe Families, "Statistics on Pornography, Sexual Addiction and Online Perpetrators," accessed April 22, 2013, http://www .safefamilies.org/sfStats.php.
7. Luke Gilkerson, Breaking Free Blog, "3 Reasons It's Not Okay to Use Porn to Spice Things Up in the Bedroom," February 3, 2012, CovenantEyes.com, http://www.covenanteyes .com/2012/02/03/3-reasons-its-not-okay-to-use-porn-to-spice -things-up-in-the-bedroom.

PASSION PRINCIPLE #3:
CELEBRATE THE EMOTIONAL SIDE OF SEX

MOVING BEYOND ABUSE
1. "Famous Failures" video, accessed April 22, 2013, http://www .youtube.com/watch?v=Y6hz_s2XIAU.

MOVING BEYOND BETRAYAL
1. Holly Holladay's blog can be found at www.hollyholladay.org.

EVOLUTION OF A RELATIONSHIP

1. Gary Thomas, *The Sacred Marriage* (Grand Rapids, MI: Zondervan, 2002), 13.
2. Holly Holladay, "Part 5: On the Other Side," *Desperately Seeking Holly* (blog) June 10, 2011, http://www.hollyholladay .org/2011/06/10/part-5-on-the-other-side/.
3. *Wikipedia*, s.v. "Fight-or-flight response," accessed April 22, 2013, http://en.wikipedia.org/wiki/Fight-or-flight_response.
4. Gary D. Chapman, *The 5 Love Languages* (Chicago: Northfield, 2009).
5. James C. Dobson and Shirley Dobson, *Night Light: A Devotional for Couples* (Colorado Springs: Multnomah, 2000), 12–13.

PASSION PRINCIPLE #4:

CELEBRATE THE PHYSICAL SIDE OF SEX

EUREKA!

1. Donald Zimmer, "Most Sensitive Spots & More," AskMen.com, accessed April 22, 2013, http://www.askmen.com/dating /dzimmer/4.html.
2. "External genital changes in fetus development," Baby2see.com, accessed April 22, 2013, http://www.baby2see.com/gender /external_genitals.html.
3. Tina S. Miracle, Andrew W. Miracle, and Roy F. Baumeister, *Human Sexuality: Meeting Your Basic Needs* (Upper Saddle River, NJ: Prentice Hall, 2003), 33.
4. Shannon Ethridge, *The Sexually Confident Wife* (New York: Three Rivers, 2009), 102–14.
5. Excerpted from Shannon Ethridge, *Every Woman's Marriage* (Colorado Springs: WaterBrook, 2006), 185–86.
6. Miracle, Miracle, and Baumeister, *Human Sexuality: Meeting Your Basic Needs*, 90.
7. Ibid., 30.
8. Ibid., 33.
9. Natalie Angier, *Woman: An Intimate Geography* (New York: Anchor Books, 1999), 63.

LET FREEDOM RING!

1. *Wikipedia*, s.v. "missionary position," accessed April 22, 2013, http://en.wikipedia.org/wiki/Missionary_position.
2. Linda Dillow and Lorraine Pintus, *Intimate Issues: Twenty-One Questions Christian Women Ask About Sex* (Colorado Springs: WaterBrook, 1999), 200.
3. Douglas E. Rosenau, *A Celebration of Sex: A Guide to Enjoying God's Gift of Sexual Intimacy* (Nashville: Thomas Nelson, 2002), 158.
4. This section adapted from Shannon Ethridge, *The Sexually Confident Wife* (New York: Three Rivers Press, 2009), 206–9.

About the Author

SHANNON ETHRIDGE IS A BEST-SELLING AUTHOR, INTERNATIONAL speaker, and certified life coach with a master's degree in counseling/human relations from Liberty University. She is the author of twenty books, including the million-copy best-selling *Every Woman's Battle* series, the five-book *Completely His* series, and *The Sexually Confident Wife*.

Shannon is a frequent guest on television and radio programs, such as *The Today Show*, *The 700 Club*, *New Life Live!* with Stephen Arterburn, and *Life Today* with James and Betty Robison. She also mentors aspiring writers and speakers through her B.L.A.S.T. program (Building Leaders, Authors, Speakers, and Teachers). Shannon lives in Tyler, Texas, with her husband, Greg, and their children, Erin and Matthew.

Learn more at www.ShannonEthridge.com.

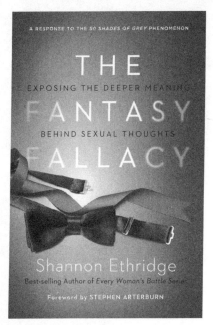

E rotica has invaded more than our minds—it has exploded onto our bestseller lists and into our bedrooms. Best-selling author Shannon Ethridge believes fantasies have deep psychological roots and, if acted on, many of them can do deep psychological damage. Let's take out the sting and allow the Lord to heal us from the insecurities and brokenness that cause inappropriate fantasies to haunt us. *The Fantasy Fallacy* includes resources for providing a safe haven for recovery, along with tips that help us (and others) recognize and heal deep emotional pain.

J ulia Whittaker's rocky past yielded two daughters, both given up for adoption as infants. Now Julia must find them to try to save her son. Can she muster the courage to face her choices and their consequences and find any hope of healing?

To Know You is Shannon Ethridge's first novel—a powerful story of reconciliation, romance, and redemption. Shannon brings to life the intense struggles women face to overcome their sexual and emotional hurdles and become the women and wives God created them to be.

THOMAS NELSON
Since 1798

Available
in print
and e-book